THE
PARADOX
PLANET

THE PARADOX PLANET

CREATING BRAND EXPERIENCES for THE AGE OF I

Larry Light *and* Joan Kiddon

Copyright © 2017 Larry Light and Joan Kiddon.

All rights reserved. No part of this book may be used or reproduced by any means, graphic, electronic, or mechanical, including photocopying, recording, taping or by any information storage retrieval system without the written permission of the author except in the case of brief quotations embodied in critical articles and reviews.

This book is a work of non-fiction. Unless otherwise noted, the author and the publisher make no explicit guarantees as to the accuracy of the information contained in this book and in some cases, names of people and places have been altered to protect their privacy.

Archway Publishing books may be ordered through booksellers or by contacting:

Archway Publishing
1663 Liberty Drive
Bloomington, IN 47403
www.archwaypublishing.com
1 (888) 242-5904

Because of the dynamic nature of the Internet, any web addresses or links contained in this book may have changed since publication and may no longer be valid. The views expressed in this work are solely those of the author and do not necessarily reflect the views of the publisher, and the publisher hereby disclaims any responsibility for them.

Any people depicted in stock imagery provided by Thinkstock are models, and such images are being used for illustrative purposes only.
Certain stock imagery © Thinkstock.

ISBN: 978-1-4808-4685-2 (sc)
ISBN: 978-1-4808-4683-8 (hc)
ISBN: 978-1-4808-4684-5 (e)

Library of Congress Control Number: 2017907320

Print information available on the last page.

Archway Publishing rev. date: 7/13/2017

ACKNOWLEDGMENTS

Arcature, our consulting company, began twenty-eight years ago. Over the course of the decades, we have had the opportunity to work with remarkable people across many different organizations around the world. This book could not have been written without their support of our ideas, principles, and processes. Some of our client relationships were public, such as our work with Mars, Nissan, McDonald's and IHG. Most remain "nameless" but cherished nevertheless. We are eternally grateful for the depth and breadth of the projects in which we participated, and the people with whom we worked.

As always, we thank our families who bring us great joy. Joyce, Michelle, Laura, Jim; Olivia, Chloé, Alex, and Naomi.

CONTENTS

Introduction	xi
PART 1: THE PARADOX PLANET	1
The Age of I	5
The Collision of Globalizing, Localizing and Personalizing	12
What Does this Mean for Brands?	16
Summary	18
PART 2: THE PARADOX PLANET'S PARADOXES	21
Connection and Disconnection	21
Alone and Together	24
Delay and Desire	27
Timeliness and Timelessness	30
Abundant and Rare	34
Exclusive and Affordable	36
Personalization (automated) and Personal (human)	38
Privacy and Personalization	41
Preserving Anonymity and Wanting to Be Known	41
Technological Control and Human Control	45
Indulgence and Wellness	51
Improved Me and Improved We	56
Innovative and Dependable	62
Technology and Comfort	63

The Three Dimensions of Ease	65
Ease of choice	65
Ease of use	67
Ease of mind	70
Safe and Adventure	72
Summary	76
Paradoxes for Paradox Promise Solutions	76

PART 3: PRINCIPLES FOR FINDING PARADOXES AND GENERATING PARADOX PROMISES *79*

1. Look for the little things	80
Newspaper: Being New and Time-Honored Every Day	80
Camel: Belong to the World and Be Solitary	81
2. Look for ideas outside of your standard social media circles, favorite periodicals, e-zines, information sites and journals	82
Chocolate Fill Bar: Fill the Hunger-Hole in Your Stomach without Being Filling	83
McDonald's: Forever and Young	84
3. Differentiate information from trends from insights	85
Crowne Plaza WorkLife Room: Be Comfortable While Being Highly Productive	87
European Appliance Company: Silent and Powerful	88
4. There is no formula for creative thinking	90
Toy Company: Safe Play and Brilliant Creativity	91
A Process for Creativity? Formulated Creativity	92
5. Ask "is this actionable?"	94
Smart Home: Being Ahead of Time in the Present	95
Apple Candy: Making a Soft Caramelized Apple Candy	96
6. Be a runway not a control tower	96
The Brand Academy: New Ideas and Business As Usual	98
Too Much Change: New is Usual	98
7. Fight the hypnosis of the measurement mystique	99
The 85% Rule: Change without Changing	101

    How to Smile: Process and Personable   102
    One Million Dollars a Customer: Make-Believe and Metrics   102
  8. Do not fall for the killer question   103
    Industrial Problem Detection: Simple and Multi-faceted   104
    Japanese Luxury Vehicle: Old is New   105
  9. You can't hurry love   106
    McDonald's: Forever Young   106
    The Role of Culture: Big and Fast   107
  Summary   108

PART 4: LESSONS FROM CREATING PARADOX PROMISES   111
  Lessons   111
    Lesson 1: Importance of the Paradox Promise   111
    Lesson 2: Importance of Freedom within a Framework   113
    Lesson 3: Importance of Organizational Diversity of Thinking   115
    Lesson 4: Importance of Collaboration   116
    Lesson 5: Importance of Discipline   118
    Lesson 6: Importance of Strategic Dexterity   119
    Lesson 7: Importance of Marketing   120
    Lesson 8: Importance of Standing Up for what you Stand For   122
    Lesson 9: Importance of Internal Marketing   124
    Lesson 10: Importance of Trust   126
    Lesson 11: Importance of Trustworthy Brand Value™   127
  Summary   129

Conclusion   131
Endnotes   133
Index   145

INTRODUCTION

For those who do not remember, or those who never saw the 1976 movie, *Network*[1], the anti-hero Howard Beale was the unstable, past his prime television anchor person who asked viewers to vent their frustration and anger about life by sticking their heads out of their windows to scream, "I'm mad as hell, and I'm not going to take this any more!" In the rant that turned him into a troubled American modern-day prophet, he exhorted his viewers with a dystopian view of life riddled with crime, fear of the Russians, rampant inflation, and a huge defense budget:

> "… You've got to get mad. You've got to say, '… My life has value.' … I want you to get out of your chairs and go to the window. Right now. I want you to go to the window and open it, and stick your head out and yell, 'I'm mad as hell, and I'm not going to take this any more!'"[2]

On the surface, it is a movie about the media, and the extent to which it would go to achieve ratings success. However, the writer Paddy Chayefsky brought to the surface the aggrieved and unsatisfied feelings people were having with life, as they knew it. He noticed the way in which the media focused on people's desires for life as it used to be when things were happier. He observed the ways in which the elite media moguls doing big media deals patronized the audience, and played on their fears and unease. He saw the impending growth of the media conglomerate. He ultimately voiced what it was like to feel utterly voiceless. Forty years ago, he recognized that people were angry. He seemed to say that anger was a part of America now, and that we had better get used to this. If, at the time, we thought the movie was a one-off, we were wrong.

1976 was a fairly ordinary time after the chaos of the Sixties, and the sins of Watergate. However, the year had its fair share of events:

- Palestinians hijacked an Air France plane, landing it at the Entebbe airport in Uganda, putting the name Idi Amin in our vocabulary.
- The rescue by Israeli forces of the hijacked Air France passengers.
- Patricia Hearst was convicted of armed robbery giving some closure to the Symbionese Liberation Army's revolutionary tactics.
- The government in Vietnam united North and South into a single Communist entity.
- We and our allies and foes continued to test nuclear missiles.
- Jimmy Carter beat Gerald Ford in the Presidential election letting us know that a "common peanut farmer" could rise to the highest office.
- The first commercial Concorde flight took place, giving the jet set and busy corporate executives a way to actually save time.

Those times seem so far away and disconnected from our world today. Apple had just been created. Today, its products, brand, and design philosophy are ubiquitous in our homes, pockets, and hands. And yet, Mr. Chayefsky saw beneath the surface, saw the simmering anger, and pulled the curtain away for all of us to see and feel it too. And, we do, now.

Author Gregg Easterbrook writes that in our current times "pessimism is mainstream: optimism is uncool." In his observation of society, he relates the paradox of 1) the disconnect between America's actual situation, which is pretty good, and, 2) the dark, disastrous, assumed awfulness of life. In other words, he observes the paradox that life is actually getting better while people are increasingly feeling lousy.[3]

Pankaj Mishra calls this, *Age of Anger: A History of The Present*. He examines the foundational theories and philosophies that engendered all of this resentment, antagonism, and, in many cases, rage. Going back to the Enlightenment, he finds the footprints that lead to where we are today.[4] Whether or not you wish to blame Voltaire and his compatriots for our anger as the book suggests, it is important to understand how the extraordinary surge of technology, digitization, 24/7 timelessness, and boundless interconnectedness have generated frustration and unbalance.

Many blame the culture of social media, which has astounding benefits but also allows people to isolate themselves with other people who think as they do viewing news and opinions that reflect and reinforce what they already believe. Social media has the ability to generate a "feeling of profound alienation."[5] Individual furor, conspiracies, hatred, and madness à la Howard Beale disciples not only brings individuals together but can cause anxiety, fear, and loathing.[6] As of this writing, we speculate on whether Germany, and Italy will have their Howard Beale moments in 2017. In the recent elections, The Netherlands and France rejected the turn towards anger. In America, we, and many others continue to speculate on the trajectory of our angry nation.

Trained to observe, synthesize and give advice, we have spent many years examining the evolution of this anger that has spurred a global malaise of polarization. We looked at the societal changes, and global, local, and personal forces that have, and still are affecting people. We followed the profusion of choices that create zero-sum situations, which have generated tensions that erupt into unrequited anger. We trace the patterns of behavior from the 1950's, Age of We, through the 1960's and 1970's, Age of Me, to today where we are living in what we call The Age of I. We do this through the lens of marketers. As marketers, these changes are critical not just for building and managing brands but also for how enterprises organize for brand leadership.

One thing is clear: over time, people have become more demanding customers, more informed customers, and more uncompromising customers. We do not accept trade-offs. Asking us to live in a zero-sum world where have to give up something we want, in order to get another something we want is no longer acceptable. Trade-offs create frustration. Frustration breeds anger.

In a world of instant gratification, where all happens in real time at any time around the clock, we want what we want when we want it. Whether it is technological advancements or other winds of change, today, we have the strong desire to have our needs met without having to compromise. Losing out is as frustrating as missing out, which sends fear into Millennials and Generation Z.

We live in a world of paradoxes. We see these paradoxical desires in cries for less government money spent on universal programs while not making any changes to our Social Security or our Medicare. We want a good-paying job in today's technologically advanced marketplace *and* want to use our current skill set. We want to belong to a nation *and* want to be valued for our individuality. We want to belong to a union of countries *and* want to keep our nationality. We want low interest rates so we can buy a house *and* we want higher interest for our savings accounts. We extol the First Amendment *and* also want to eliminate language we find offensive.

We live in a world of contradictions. In today's social, economic, political, institutional, personal and business environment, finding solutions to address contradictory needs helps create and build value for customers, shareholders, employees and other stakeholders. Otherwise, the forces of conflicting needs and wants will pull us apart. How we address our conflicts will have a major and tumultuous affect on business, and brands in particular.

A brief perusal of David Brooks' columns in *The New York Times* shows just how contradictory and paradoxical our society is: in January

2016, he wrote of "The Movement Mentality: the forces of individualism that are atomizing intellectual life and the tendency to define ourselves by our academic disciplines or by gender or racial groups rather than by philosophy or shared vision;" in May 2016, he wrote about our "Fragmented Society – an age of decentralization and fragmentation… we attach ourselves to looser more flexible networks instead of larger established institutions;" and "One Community At a Time" saying that "our central challenge is social isolation which is starting the rise of intentional community instigators." And, these are just a few.[7]

This book is about the imperative of maximizing conflicting needs. It is about the conflicted world in which we live, our Paradox Planet, where we must optimize contrary desires through integration rather than compromise. We believe that two major trends have created the Paradox Planet: The Age of I, and, The Collision of Globalizing, Localizing, and Personalizing Forces.

We examine how many successful brands and businesses understood contrary needs, and then created compelling Paradox Promises where customers did not have to trade off desired benefits. Delivering a Paradox Promise means making a better, new whole from the combination of two or more entities.

The book has four parts.

- In Part 1, we look at the two trends: The Age of I and The Collision of Globalizing, Localizing and Personalizing forces. We describe the Paradox Planet, and how we got here.
- In Part 2, we describe the myriad of contradictions where people do not want to trade off, providing examples of institutions, businesses and brands that did, and do this well.
- In Part 3, we provide principles for managing for success in the Paradox Planet.
- And, in Part 4, we share lessons for creating Paradox Promises.

Whether in politics, economics, society, relationships or brand experiences, in a world of paradoxes aiming for balance will not foster profitable success. Balance means viewing paradoxes as constant sum contests: 50 percent of one thing and 50 percent of another. More of one desire means accepting less of another. This is not today's reality.

The Paradox Planet is a marketing lesson with broader application. We see the desire for satisfaction of conflicting needs as important for all institutions. Opting to deliver Paradox Promises has implications for all institutions, not just brands and businesses. There are repercussions across geography and societal, institutional organizations.

Although 2016 was the Howard Beale global moment, it is not something that instantly appeared fully formed. It had been in the works for some time. This book looks at the past, and, how we can manage today, and in the future, in an increasingly polarized world. Acknowledging the benefits of diversity, we also believe that we can find commonalities by addressing frustrations and anger with promises that provide compelling, cohesive maximization of divergent desires.

PART 1

THE PARADOX PLANET

We live in a world of contradictions. Polarization has a firm grasp on our institutions and our beliefs. After the Brexit vote in the United Kingdom, and the recent 2016 American presidential election, pundits, sociologists, commentators, and historians have commented on the ways in which nations are polarized. Discussions on populism and how it is dividing developed nations are the theme of many current analyses. There are many points of view on how many developed and developing countries have populations that live in parallel societies.[8] Fostered by demographics, technology, immigration, an increasingly borderless business environment, and the anxiety of living in a rapidly changing world, the pull of identity politics is overpowering the need for unity. Alienation, feeling voiceless relative to a circle of elite, global financiers, and CEOs has united groups of people into a powerful political force.

The effects of the 2008 recession left a lasting impression that has for many meant living in a world of uncertainty. There was a great unraveling, with many people experiencing a great sense of loss: loss of ownership, loss of wealth, loss of savings, loss of comfort, loss of security, and a loss of trust. Uncertainty covers all sorts of emotions such as bewilderment, anxiety and doubt. We are skeptical and distrusting. Our world seems unsettled, unpredictable, and unstable. Our leaders and institutions are inconsistent, indecisive, and unsure.

We feel apprehensive and precarious. As the world became more connected, more technologically and digitally savvy, with melting borders, virtual communities, and shifting values, there is this loss of control. *The 2016 Edelman Trust Barometer* indicates that after years of declining institutional trust, there is now an "inequality in trust," what it terms a "significant divide in trust."[9]

The recent WEF Davos event dedicated a panel called *The Crisis of the Middle Class*, which segued into a heated discussion on populism and how to deal with its ramifications,[10] as if the issue of populism and elitism had never been raised during the previous Davos in 2016. In January 2016, Martin Wolf, Gideon Rachman, and Michael Skapinker, all for *Financial Times*, warned about the pending, possible revolt of the "ordinary people" against a Davos elite in incredibly prescient ways. As Martin Wolf wrote,

> "... Ordinary people, notably native-born men, are alienated. They feel used and abused. ... They see elites as incompetent and predatory. The surprise is not that many are angry but that so many are not."[11]

What has emerged is a world where people do not want to compromise anymore. We are unwilling to trade off. And, we become angry when we have to, especially when it favors an environment where we perceive the deck is stacked against us. Although the most visible expressions of this polarization are in politics, the facts are that polarization affects business and brands. Angry, frustrated people take their emotions out not just on politicians and other leaders but also on companies.

Data from The Futures Company's *Global Monitor*, a globally-run, annual survey, indicated four years ago, in a 2013 report that people who consider themselves "enraged" stopped buying products and services from global brands, and thought less favorably of global brands. Among the "Global Enraged" 47 percent were angry that, "Big business maximizes profit at the expense of community and consumers," and, 45 percent were angry that, "Business and corporations have more influence on government policy than citizens do." Additionally, supporting the rise of populism, *Global Monitor* reported that over half of its respondents expressed anger over the feeling that, "Too much money is concentrated in the hands of too few people." And, 50 percent of those interviewed were angry that the elites live by rules that are different from the rest of us, clearly a basis for the intense, current emotions around inequality. One can understand that these responses reflected an increasingly skeptical global audience that was fuming and, as Howard Beale would say, mad. Part of the systemic, global anger stems from the recognition that we live in a world of declining traditions and values, which is the lack of bonding that David Brooks talks about: a lack of personal and social connections; patronage built on success, not on hard work; and the overwhelming sense that politicians are incompetent or corrupt.[12]

The data from *Global Monitor* should have been a blueprint and a wake up call. Many companies buy these data. These statements are tracked annually and yet it would seem that institutions did not pay attention. Furthermore, our institutional reactions have been to appease one side while frustrating the other side. This failure to maximize the polarities creates a hyperpolarized landscape.

In today's social, economic, political, institutional, personal, and business environment, addressing conflicting needs helps create and build value for people, customers, shareholders, employees, and other institutional and corporate stakeholders. The forces of contradictory needs and wants are pulling us apart. How we address our conflicts will have a major and tumultuous effect on business, and brands in particular.

Managing and succeeding with paradoxes is a frequently reviewed leadership dimension. "Understanding paradox may hold a key to coping with, and even excelling in the face of strategic tensions."[13] Creative tensions are strategic drivers. Identified in 1994 as the "Tyranny of the OR" by Collins and Porras, they point out that the trade-off approach is less likely to produce high performance and that going for the "Genius of the AND" is a hallmark of successful, visionary organizations.[14]

Research indicates that in start-up companies, the first blush of development focus is singular, that is, a deliberate trade-off. But, after these initial moments, the focus is on solving a paradox. As the venture becomes more entrenched, the choice of a paradox strategy tends to occur.

> "… A paradoxical approach aims at choosing A and B simultaneously. Although the options may seem contradictory, their interrelations often allow for their coexistence. Thus, the goal of a paradoxical approach is to present a both/and solution, emphasizing common grounds and contrasts of the opposing elements."[15]

In our current environment, whether personal, political or business, people appear to be rejecting trade-off solutions (choose X or Y) that make them feel they have made a poor decision. They also seem to be rejecting UN resolution-type decisions that compromise X and Y to create a Z solution: a revision to X and Y that creates an agreeable but tepid Z, a solution about which we cannot be passionate. Humans do not like making bad decisions.[16] Forcing a trade-off or watering down two options to make a third option comes across as a bad decision. Bad decisions are painful, and if anything, we are pain avoidance mammals.

Studies focused on choice reveal that trade-off decisions reflect conflicts. Some conflicts are more emotionally charged than others. Trade-off decisions generate negative emotions. The decision-maker may sense a threat to achieving a goal. The decision-maker may feel that something of value will have to be lost in this process. One result is that the decision-maker may avoid having to decide. This avoidance mechanism is usually associated with high-difficulty choices. Through avoidance, the decision-maker does not have to deal with loss aversion.[17]

In an uncertain, volatile world, difficult choices can appear to be more challenging and threatening to personal stability. These trade-offs may require too much personal justification for not enough benefit. Rather than having to choose or accept a lesser solution, today we seek the maximization of contrary needs. It defines our world, the Paradox Planet.

From our perspective and learning, there are two major influences that have created, and continue to create this situation, 1) The Age of I, and, 2) The Collision of Globalizing, Localizing and Personalizing.

The Age of I

"The Age of I" refers to the tension between two strong human desires: the need to belong (inclusivity) *and* the need to have a unique identity (individualism). It is an overarching paradox that drives our attitudes and behaviors. We want to be seen and respected as individuals with special characteristics, but also we want to belong to something bigger: a community, a network, a business, a family, an ethnic group, a religious institution, a union, or a nation. We want to be independent *and* interdependent at the same time.

Having to trade off between these two innate desires, being an individual and belonging to a group, is an emotionally difficult decision as both are essential. Social behavior research suggests that both independence and belonging are essential for finding and securing our place in life.[18] And, sociologists, psychologists, behaviorists, and those who study culture articulate the power of the independent self and the interdependent self, and the ways in which these interact. The personal self and the social self "mutually reinforce each other."[19]

In our digital, networked, mobile environment, increasingly, we find that we can be ourselves *and* be part of group at the same time. We can easily find digital and virtual ways to experience both of these desires simultaneously. And, ubiquitous technology and online communities allow us to create different social identities depending on the group in which we are participating. Individuals defining who they are and what they want to be can have multiple identities depending on the social network.

A recent paper discusses the effect of multiple "accessible selves" that float from social network to social network. In The Age of I, a person's self-identity and her social selves constantly interact for achieving self-identity. The individual wants to be herself but at the same time her self is also shaped by interactions with others. This impacts brands as well as corporations.[20] It seems that when interacting, online or in a loyalty program, for example, individuality and brand community affect a brand's identity, especially when individuals within the brand's community actively work on behalf of the brand.[21]

Customers have the ability to individualize a brand experience, and also share the brand experience with various global, regional and local "communities" of like-minded others to which they choose to belong. As a frequent Starbuck's customer, you may belong to their loyalty program's group but your favorite coffee or other beverage is uniquely created to your own individual tastes. And, if you are a "vocal" and ardent member of the Starbuck's online community, you might find yourself co-creating on behalf of the brand. Your ideas and comments will have an affect on the brand's reputation and identity.

Technology has also reinforced the paradoxical nature of The Age of I in the ways in which we relate, or do not relate, to others. Jacob Bernstein reported in *The New York Times* that wearing headphones in a crowd on the subway or walking down the street is a modern paradox of "alone together," living in the crowd without personal interaction.[22] In his column on technology, Christopher Mims extolled the social app Houseparty that allows teens (Gen Z) to have a virtual social event via a group video chat. The app is for hanging out with friends something they say they do less frequently than they used to do.[23] Hanging out with friends on your phone is an example of technology affecting the need to be an individual and belong to a group. Kids can be their unique selves and part of the group. As one young Millennial said to us, " I want to be different just like all my friends."

We are social animals: sometimes, virtual communities are not enough. As pointed out in an article about the 2017 SXSW Festival, we may opt for digital music that can be individualized for each person's preferences with streams, pods, and personalized content apps, but we still crave the actual, human, in-person, "joy" of shared belonging generated by the live, collective concert.

> "At a time when the music business and the tech companies that now dominate it are concentrating on a customized experience, SXSW shows how much people still prize a communal one."[24]

WeWork, a creator and provider of communal office space is a perfect example of The Age of I addressing the desire to work for oneself and the desire to be part of an "office" community. The mission and founding narrative on the WeWork website, says,

> "Work to make a life, not just a living. When we started WeWork in 2010, we wanted to build more than beautiful, shared office spaces. We wanted to build a community. A place you join as an individual, 'me', but where you become part of a greater 'we'."[25]

The ability to personalize services and products allows people to have it their way while belonging to a community. At one chain hotel, the mini bar was filled with Diet Coke because the guest preferred that beverage. The overall service was standard but there was this gift of catering to the guest's personal needs.

In the 1950's, it was an era of conformity. People wanted what everyone else had. There was no benefit to being different. People wanted the same cars in the driveway, the same house in the same development, the same soup cans and cake mixes in the cupboard. People commuted on the same trains, wore the same suits, and, came home at the same time. There were hardly any varieties of family units as there are today. Commonality was key. People even desired the same avocado green kitchen appliances. The comfort of familiarity reigned after the trauma of World War II. Mass products and services were mass marketed, and mass distributed, to mass markets through mass advertising in mass media. Having a television in increasing numbers of households helped. Belonging was everything. It has been suggested[26] that the recent United States' election (and, one could say the Brexit vote) is a wish to transport the country back to the 1950s. This is described as an enforced stability negating the "go west" vitality and spirit that, in fact, made America, and made it great.

As the children of these 1950s households grew up, the response to conformity was individuality to the extreme. In the 1960's and 1970's, it was "all about me." "Let me do my own thing." "What's in it for me?" This was the era of hippies, flower children, Woodstock, the summer of love, the acid tests: a time of consciousness-raising, self-focused, self-absorbed, self-actualizing "me-ness." The focus on sheer independence created marketing that catered to a self-centered, self-interested, self-obsessed group of young people. The consciousness-raising program est (Erhard Seminars Training, developed and led by Werner Erhard) was the therapy of choice. People increasingly looked inside of selves. Non-conformity, breaking with the past, anti-establishment, rejection of family values and structure, led us to focus on the importance of differences.

The happy 1960's ended abruptly with the tragic devolution at Altamont outside of San Francisco in 1969, although there were prior events that pointed to this sad end, such as the May 1969 debacle at the People's Park in Berkeley. The killings at Kent State sealed the demise. When we woke up, we were in the self-destructiveness age of disco, drugs and decadence defining the 1970's. It was what Thomas Hine calls, "The Great Funk" in his book of the same name describing, *Falling Apart and Coming Together (on a shag rug) in the Seventies.*[27] The divisiveness of the 1960's with the personal liberations, the Vietnam War, and the ascension of Richard Nixon lit the fire of anger and frustration that has continued to simmer even during the "morning in America" Reagan era.

As we pointed out in a one of our previous books, *New Brand Leadership*, the way we communicated to people through advertising celebrated our individuality.

> "Advertising during the "age of me" reflected this "me mentality." Now defunct Braniff Airlines ran an ad featuring Andy Warhol and Sonny Liston using Liston's mantra: 'If you got it, flaunt it.' Nice 'N Easy Hair Color said, 'It let's me be me.' Hertz said, 'Hertz puts you in the driver's seat.'"[28]

In that same book, we quote the historian Richard Miller who commented on the 1960's by saying that time was about freedom, which he described as "the absence of physical, mental, emotional, cultural, and even biological restraint…. This idea… is Autonomy."[29]

Today's era is different. People want both "we" and "I," distinctiveness and belonging. Instead of the Sixties mantra of a world revolving around me, now I want a world that includes, understands, respects, and recognizes me. I want to stand out from the crowd while simultaneously I want to be part of the crowd, conforming to the community of the crowd. I want to be in the crowd and apart from the crowd. I want a sense of "intimacy" combined with "isolation", as journalist Bernstein reports, the "paradox of the headphone experience."[30] I want independence with interconnection. Individual commonalities are important. I want to be unique and I want to share my uniqueness with like-minded people. The self-obsessed counter culture has morphed into the selfie-celeb connected culture. We live in a web of networked individualism, or networked narcissism.

When there is no group with which to share, we become unmoored. Belonging is an innate human desire. As described by Marcia Pally, a professor at NYU and Fordham, we seek "separability and situatedness." We want the freedom to be creative and independent, yet we need the embrace and engagement of the group, whether a family, a culture, a community or a nation.[31]

However, in The Age of I, much of the self and much of the community are digital. Our identity and belonging have become clickable not touchable. An inherent paradox of the independent/connected force of The Age of I is the tension between our real selves and our digital selves, and between our real families and our digital families. The latter is changing the nature of how we view and describe family.

Putting aside the multiple possibilities of the modern family unit and gender (traditional, single-hood, non-marital cohabitation, single parent, remarried or step-parent, foster or adoptive, childless, empty nest, multi-adult, non-secretive-extra marital, multi-generational), due to technology, we now have families that are kin and families that are kindred. Kin families are our familial connections, through blood or bonded arrangement, while kindred families are our families based on communities, networks and circles in which we participate.[32] I may be a different individual depending on the family group: who I am now depends on with whom and where I may be. In The Age of I, social structures are expanded: there are multiple opportunities for individuals to gain inclusivity.

A recent trend in the United States is the development of monastic-type, faith-based communities (See "The Benedict Option" in *The Wall Street Journal*)[33] that wish to separate themselves from the wider world. Such movements are not alien to the country as the Amish still live in their own spaces, and, there are still "intentional" communities evolved from the 1960s communes. Separating from the values of society to be with like-minded others whether it is around a monastery, or around a gated golf club, or segregated communities of shared values, reflects the tension of The Age of I to belong as a member where I (and my family) can behave according to our values without interference.

The societal implications of The Age of I represent multiple opportunities for institutions. Finding solutions that maximize contradictory needs is difficult but not impossible. For example, think about the issues regarding the European Union. Although some member states are frustrated with the European Union, they understand its founding concept and recognize its potential advantages. There is nothing wrong in principle with belonging to a union of European countries. Belonging has its benefits. Union has efficiencies. Connectedness is meaningful. On the other hand, preserving national identity including national laws, national cuisine, and the national ethos is critical. From the standpoint of the critics, the EU governance became a zero-sum situation, which appeared to favor the union rather than the nation. By necessity, balancing interests leads to compromise, and compromise leads to less of everything, similar to a United Nation resolution. More union can lead to less nationhood, or a different kind of nationhood. The perceptions, and possibly the reality in some cases, were that the union was performing against the best interests of the individual countries. And some nations saw elements of their national identity and culture being diminished or damaged under the powerful, governing rubric of the union. This may sound simplistic but it is not, it is difficult: figuring out how to maximize the individuality of the countries and the inclusivity of the union must be a priority if the EU is meant to survive. People want to trade up not trade off.

The Age of I is not a mere marketing idea: it is a powerful social force that we use for making marketing relevant and compelling. The Age of I is, in and of itself, a forceful paradoxical influence regardless of institution, business or brand. As such, it drives numerous other paradoxes creating a paradoxical world. The current arguments about globalization (global economy) and isolation (domestic needs) is an example of the tension between belonging to something bigger, outside of borders, and independence, inside of borders. Should we have open borders or should we close our doors? There is anxiety and optimism. The fears about nationalism and/or nativism are part of a conversation about separateness and solidarity.

One of the most intriguing political expressions of The Age of I came from Mark Carney, the governor of The Bank of England as he spoke about how to deal with the inequality that globalism has wrought. His proffered solution was having, "… An inclusive form of global commerce with the individual at its centre." He titled this "artisanal globalisation"[34]

To be successful in The Age of I, it is necessary to address needs-driven, occasion-based conflicts by developing compelling, trustworthy branded paradox promises that deliver relevant, differentiated (brand) experiences. But, as we stated, it is not the only influence. There is another, equally potent influence that is affecting our world, the collision of globalizing, localizing and personalizing.

The Collision of Globalizing, Localizing and Personalizing

We have written about this confluence of forces in previous books, articles, speeches and brochures. As with The Age of I, the crash of these forces is more than marketing. The implications are societal, political, and economic. Institutions and industries operate in a world where there are global needs, local needs and personal needs, which must be satisfied at the same time. And again, this confluence of forces must be optimally integrated rather than balanced, which as we have said, is a zero-sum situation forcing trade-off decisions that no one wants to make. Maximization of these conflicting forces can be messy: it is easier to opt for trade-offs.

We experience the influence of these three forces every day. For example, the car we drive is assembled from parts that flow over a global supply chain. That car was purchased, and is serviced, at a local dealership that is part of the community. In fact, many dealerships use the town's or the city's name in their titles. The car's colors, options, and other add-ons were personalized to match the owner's whims, albeit from a standard set of choices.

A hotel that is a part of a chain has global standards for safety and hygiene. It also reflects the manners and behaviors of the local country, and/or neighborhood in which it resides. In Asia, the business card will be held and offered respectfully with two hands. The menu will have locally-grown foods or regional tastes. And, your service may be personalized, especially if that hotel recognizes you as a frequent guest, or as a member of its loyalty program.

The Publix Supermarket[35] in your hometown is part of a larger over-arching organizational entity with many standards and a common ESOP program (Employee Stock Ownership Plan). But, each store will have different items to reflect the local neighborhood's tastes and purchase behaviors. A store in a largely Hispanic-Caribbean neighborhood carries a wide selection of Jamaican foods, and South American peppers and seasonings. Again, the stores are also designed to provide personalization through special ordering, delivery, and relationships with the people behind the counter, and the wine "sommelier."

As a marketing process and mind-set, being global has evolved over the decades. In *New Brand Leadership*[36], we trace the evolution of global marketing from 1) complete standardization to 2) "Think Global, Act Local" to 3) The Collaborative Three-Box Model that helps brands organize for success in a global, local and personal world. The principles of *New Brand Leadership* are important. These principles help multi-nationals establish and systematize an approach for leveraging the challenges of global, local and personal. Enterprises with global brands have to manage in a business environment that requires maximizing the three forces. It used to be simpler.

In the 1980's, the common thinking was to have one standard, global positioning for a single, globally standardized product or service that was supported by a single expression and execution of this brand positioning. Proposed by Harvard professor Theodore Levitt, corporations established a centralized marketing structure that managed all external and internal marketing. Local satellites existed to execute the global strategies and tactics. The global-central approach left nothing to chance. And, because it was so cost efficient, it was very popular. It placed all control in the center. British Airways used this approach in its successful campaign, "The World's Favourite Airline" when it made its transition from state-owned BOAC to BA.

In the January 28, 2017 issue of *The Economist*, this decades-old approach of standardization is discussed as the precursor to some of today's perceptions of what it means to be a global company. Using KFC and McDonald's as examples, the writer states the concept: "global firms, run by global managers and owned by global shareholders should sell global products to global customers."[37]

When Professor Levitt introduced the idea of standardized, centralized, one theme marketing, he believed that local differences were passé, the left-over residue of a past world of national fractionalization that brought the world to the precipice twice in WWI and WWII. He fervently believed in global homogeneity that would blanket the planet generating power and profitability. However, as efficient and effective as the globalized, centralized, homogenized approach was, it fostered an environment of what we call "basic common denominator" thinking where ideas are pleasingly tolerable everywhere and especially relevant nowhere.

As the 1980's transitioned into the 1990's the conversations within organizations revolved around how to make the leadership and management of global brands more sensitive to local/regional cultures. Organizations searched for ways in which brand promises could be both globally standardized and locally relevant and differentiated. The resulting mantra that led to a revised approach was Think Global. Act Local. (TGAL).

As a phrase, it captured the two prevailing sides of the dilemma. And, its execution should have been the maximization of these two antithetical positions. But instead, the global center was determined to hang on to the power. In theory, TGAL was the best way to build, and broaden, global brand appeal in local/regional ways. However, centricity won out over theory. TGAL became just another "creative" way for the center to maintain its hegemony over the local/regional offices. For those practicing TGAL, the basics were that the center did all the important thinking and creating, and then, the center handed over the thinking and creative to the regions for execution. A problem with TGAL was the avoidance of accountability in the countries. Since the regions were not involved in strategies and tactics, the hand-off model allowed the regional managers to avoid responsibility for any and all actions dictated by the center's strategy. If a strategy or a tactic failed, the regions could say that it was not their fault, as they did not develop these ideas. And, because the strategies and tactics were created in the center, there was less sensitivity to the regions than originally imagined. This allowed the corporate center to observe that any and all strategic and tactical failures were due to lack of commitment by the local geographies leading to poor local execution.

Over time, the tensions between the regions and the center became intense hindering the execution of thoughts and actions that were in the brand's best interests. And, as the world became more local with desires for local products, local tastes, local talents, and local cultures, TGAL, as executed, became less effective. This is not to say that it did not work. It did. It worked well for a time, until technology changed the equation adding personalization. Understanding how to maximize rather than balance global and local is a skill. As *The Economist* points out, "Many industries that tried to globalize seem to work best when national or regional."[38]

Our current business environment now has this third force, the force of personalizing, brought on by the unrelenting charge of technology, digitization, and the power of being interconnected. The Age of I brings individuals together but as individuals, people want to maintain their sense of identity while belonging to a community of like-minded others. Part of this sense of identity is built on local differences, cultural differences, and personal differences. Personalizing also reflects our desires for recognition, status, and respect. Research conducted in China shows that localization could build on cultural-specific elements to improve international business relationships while helping the personal level of the relationship.[39]

Marketing is now more customized, individualized, and, yes, personalized. Global brands have to contend with a three-way tug of war: how can we maintain our global, standard aspects while reflecting local relevance and complementing personal differentiation?

When maximizing the three forces of globalizing, localizing and personalizing, a global hotel chain will maintain its universal standards, reflect local culture, and make sure that your room is on the same floor as the gym because you like exercising very early in the morning. The newspapers you request will be outside your door.

Brands that deliver personalized experiences are perceived to be valuable experiences. They deliver against the individual's needs reinforcing positive feelings of self, status, and respect, and uniqueness. Personalized experiences do not need to be overly complicated, and are not only in the purview of premium brands. Clinique recently introduced make-up shades that you blend yourself (into your own makeup) so it is just your exact shade: Clinique BIY™ Blend it Yourself Pigment Drops.[40]

These two major influences: 1) The Age of I, and 2) The Collision of Globalizing, Localizing and Personalizing, are outcomes of social, economic, psychological, geographic, relational, technological evolutions, or revolutions. Both describe the paradoxical needs that people have and how people want these needs to be addressed. Both reflect a fractionated, individualized world *and* a world that seeks out coalitions and associations.

In the mid-1970s when Paddy Chayefsky wrote *Network*, he saw the negative effects of news organizations' headlong rush to anesthetize and entertain, the downside of the desire for ratings over the real, and the population's anger due to uncertainty and events outside of its control. Today, we face an environment where the elemental level of the individual combined with the magnitude of communities of like-minded others is a most powerful dynamic.

What Does this Mean for Brands?

It is no longer a cliché to say that our brand-business environment is unpredictable, unstable and in some instances, precarious. Political, economic, religious, social, financial and cultural changes and upheavals are roiling the landscape. The linear, analytic approach to management that is offered through case studies at universities cannot provide ways to deal with this particular kind of universal insecurity and constant flux. "The highly mathematical models... tend to focus more on well-defined problems rather than the messy ambiguities of the real world."[41] Brands and businesses need to integrate synthesis into the analytic cultures that are now driven by masses of data with unfettered flows of communication and information.

In this new Paradox Promise world, marketers will have to articulate and market their brands differently. Brands (organizations) must leverage Paradox Promises into brand-focused strategies and actions creating a pathway for profitability. Brands (organizations) must create extraordinary trustworthy, valued, brand experiences, driving brand decisions that customers make as individuals, and as members of communities. Brands (organizations) will need to effectively deliver these Paradox Promises in a global, local, and personal world.

Whether in politics, economics, society, relationships, or brand experiences, in a world of paradoxes, aiming for balance will not foster profitable success. Balance means viewing paradoxes as constant sum contests: fifty percent of one thing versus fifty percent of another. More of one desire means accepting less of another. This is not today's reality. Delivering a Paradox Promise solution means making a better, new whole from the combination of two or more entities.

In the context of these fundamental developments marketing must change. Success in today's environment will require building strong valuable brands in a world of contradictory needs. People want their individuality to be recognized, and they want to feel they belong to a group that shares their distinctiveness. People want to be independent and interconnected, at the same time. This is the underlying paradox affecting how we make decisions today. In the 1960's and 1970's, a time of consciousness-raising, self-absorption, personal success, self actualizing, the focus was on "me" and, "What is in it for me?" Now, people desire the maximization of inclusivity and individuality.

Customers today do not want either/or solutions. Customers expect brands and businesses to optimize conflicting needs. For short-term and long-term success, single-minded solutions will not work. The old-fashioned idea of "positioning" by aiming to own a single word in a customer's mind is outdated thinking that is destined to fail. Brands are promises of complex, multi-dimensional, multi-faceted experiences. Reducing brands to a single word is simplistic, old-think marketing.

In this new Paradox Promise landscape it is even more important to deliver a compelling, differentiating, trustworthy, multi-dimensional idea. In every category the challenge is to identify the biggest, most relevant Paradox Promise opportunity. Paradox Promises address desired yet conflicting needs by delivering the benefits of an optimized whole. Promising and delivering branded Paradox Promises generates enduring profitable growth.

Summary

- We live in a world of contradictions.
- We are angry.
- Uncertainty, anxiety, ambiguity, distrust generate proactive survival: populism defines our landscape.
- Paradox Planet is where people want contrary needs maximized.
- No trade-off is the best trade-off: a trade-off means losing something of value.
- No compromises: a compromise means creating something that is agreeable but not loved; something balanced not optimally integrated.
- Two major forces underlying the Paradox Planet: 1) The Age of I, and, 2) Collision of Globalizing, Localizing, and Personalizing.
- The Age of I: Individuality and Inclusivity, Independence and Interdependence, By Myself and Belong.

- Collision of Globalizing, Localizing, and Personalizing: from single, globally standardized to Think Global. Act Local. to globally consistent, locally relevant and personally differentiating.
- For brands this means leveraging the forces of The Age of I and globalizing, localizing, and personalizing to create branded Paradox Promises based on the optimization of contradictory needs.

PART 2

THE PARADOX PLANET'S PARADOXES

Check a newspaper, magazine, scholarly journal, or business trade press; read an e-zine, white paper investigations, or an online news aggregator; listen to podcasts, talk radio, or television news reports: we live on a Paradox Planet. Paradoxes are all around. Some brands and enterprises focus on maximizing these contradictory needs. Below we examine, and describe, numerous paradoxes using examples that we have experienced or observed. Paradoxes can be multi-dimensional. As we will describe, there may be paradoxes within the paradoxes.

CONNECTION AND DISCONNECTION

We hear over and over again that our world is hyper-connected. An event in one country is known instantaneously around the globe. Logistic systems ensure that goods are delivered in real time, any time, anywhere. We are able to connect via mobile phone, text, email, Skype, Face Time, Kik, or conference calling by pressing a button, swiping a screen or turning on a machine. We have access, and are constantly accessible. We are always on. Many retail stores are open 24/7. On the Internet, nothing is ever closed; nothing is ever secret; and waiting for the next news cycle has seen its last days. And yet, we yearn for time out, time off, and time away from the constant flow of messages, updates, photographs, and all other digital demands for our attention.

Club Med, the all inclusive, single package, vacation village resorts, is a social community. The brand communicates that its "club" is the choice when you want to

> "... Disconnect from life's daily stressors and reconnect with the ones you love. And, since everything is taken care of, you can enjoy each other without distraction."[42]

In France, there is the recognition that at some point in our day we need to separate from our work: our digital connectedness is unbalanced and overwhelming. A French "right to disconnect" law passed in January 2017, requiring companies to create new protocols for after-office-hours email including setting aside hours when one does not have to reply, and avoiding "reply all" emails.[43]

In Northern California, attending Camp Grounded means stepping off the grid at the cost of approximately $570 for 4 days. Not only do you give up your devices, you cannot talk about work. As described in *Forbes* and *The New York Times*, Camp Grounded, an adults-only summer camp organized by Digital Detox, is filled with "... professionals, yearning to trade their tech-weary life for a snippet of childhood."[44] On its website, Digital Detox® Retreats describes itself, under the headline, "Disconnect to Reconnect," as:

> "The first internationally renowned tech-free personal wellness retreat where attendees give up their smartphones and gadgets in exchange for an off-the-grid experience of growth, reflection, mindfulness, creativity, community and (dis)connection."[45]

In today's convoluted digital environment, we are so connected that we must disconnect in order to have real connections, and, a real life once again.

It used to be that we could retreat to our homes after work for solace but watching TV is now an interactive, connective, streaming activity even when we are alone. And as for work, as more and more people become part of the "gig" economy, there is no office for socializing so the job connects us to others. We may belong to a "virtual" community of Uber drivers or Airbnb renters, but we are not connected to a physical office, there is no physical social hall. WeWork and other communal office space developers are filling this void. Some hotel chains such as Marriott and Westin provide access to communal working spaces to allow business travelers to connect with others while on the road.

Andrew Sullivan, the former editor of *The New Republic*, author of articles in *Time, Atlantic, The Daily Beast*, commentator, and blogger, wrote about this paradox of connection-disconnection-reconnection in a recent *New York* (magazine) article, "I Used To Be Human." He recounts the arc of his compulsion to be "living in the web" and the physical and mental toll inflicted by unending engagement.[46] One of the points made in the article is that while we continue to amass "friends" at exponential rates, we find ourselves bereft of real interaction. Being a "contact" is not the same as being a friend.

Social media sites provide avenues for disconnected connections as we sign up to follow people who we like, who communicate to us en masse, and who we will never meet. These businesses have mastered the art of maximizing a sense of connecting while we are separated at arm's length, giving new meaning to being in the same social circles. From this virtual approach to friendship where fans are followers, we develop new ways of feeling social. There is the cultural phenomenon of "microholidays"- frequent online celebrations connecting like-minded people who otherwise might be alone. Wanting the warmth of a holiday get together, this type of connection is a response to the individual's need to belong, and to minimize the fear of missing out when we are away from our "friends" during a holiday. The paradox goes further in that everyone and anyone can celebrate Vegan Day or "Sub of the Day" Day. However, at the same time, it makes individuals recognize just how alone they are.[47]

The 1980's witnessed the rise of the "workout" culture with gyms brands popping up, ubiquitous fitness clothing stores, the ever-present Reebok shoe, and get-into-shape videos, not the least of which was Jane Fonda's videotape series. Depending on the person leading the aerobics class, some workout sessions were booked solid with no room for someone arriving late from work. Gyms provided fitness and friendships: you could meet people, hang out, or go for a coffee after a class. You were you, with your own routines, possibly your own trainer, *and,* you were also a member of a group: the gym where you belonged said something about you. Equinox, LA Fitness, and the YMCA were places for connections as well as conditioning. In fact, based on a series of articles in *Rolling Stone* magazine, the movie *Perfect,* with John Travolta and Jamie Lee Curtis (1985) looked at the LA fitness scene as places where single people could meet other single people and connect, as it were. In The Age of I, brands such as the new NordicTrack x22i Incline Trainer, Peleton, Beachbody, and ClassPass allow us to connect to fitness (live, and/or on demand programs) without leaving our homes, disconnecting us from the social aspect of working out.[48]

The ultimate optimization of connection and disconnection may be Eternime. Eternime tackles the problems of the final disconnect: it keeps you connected post-mortem using a chatbot. The chatbot is a version of you that you create prior to your demise. You imbue it with your most important thoughts, stories, and memories. This allows relatives and friends an opportunity to converse with you (albeit via your avatar) after your death.[49] Eternime gives "always on" a new meaning.

ALONE AND TOGETHER

Another way to think about **Connection and Disconnection** is **Alone and Together**, which is defined as having a lot of friends *and* feeling lonesome. Roger Cohen, who writes for *The New York Times,* observed that the desire to connect with all the people in our world leaves us stranded as posture-challenged people always "downward facing with a device-dazzled gaze."⁵⁰ Our obsession with devices and headphones keep us plugged into ourselves even when we are with other people. In restaurants, we observe diners deeply involved with their phones sometimes ignoring the others at the table. People walk on the beach with a phone glued to their ear ignoring the ocean and the birds. Airplane mode allows us to keep the connection even when we are alone in our seat.

New York (magazine) had a blurb on its "Approval Matrix" page about a researcher at the University of Chicago who revealed that the percentage of lonely Americans has doubled in the last few decades.⁵¹ The *Like* button, selfies, swiping, and fandom have not helped. This phenomenon of being with others virtually and feeling alone was discussed in *The Dartmouth* (Dartmouth College) in January 2017:

> "A paradox of the present day is that technology is drawing us closer and closer together while we seem to be growing further and further apart." The article continued by recognizing that although technology has certainly improved our ability to interconnect, "… in another sense much bad has also resulted. In the place of communication between hearts and souls has come a superficial communication."⁵²

The popularity of the television show, *This is Us*, is perceived to be due in part to the uncertainty in the United States after a grueling and divisive election. "… Nobody knows what to expect in the next couple months, coming weeks and year ahead," says one of the stars of the show. The show connects with viewers on an emotional and "cathartic" basis in similar ways as the movie *Terms of Endearment*. Viewers can see themselves; they see a family with challenges in ways that are more real than the reality of reality shows.⁵³

Our world is one of intimate isolation. The Internet has created a society of "connected aloneness" and "digital depression"⁵⁴ as people spend more time engaging in virtual worlds. We seem to be individuals in a constant search for belonging. Why is this increasing? One reason is the impermanence of our online relationships. Another is our environment of insecurity. Uncertainty breeds anxiety about the state of the world and our place in it. We fear for our safety so we hide in gated communities, multiple-lock locked doors, and we make sure our children are never walking alone. Technology allows us to be anywhere and everywhere while being nowhere. We have replaced the human voice and conversation with mini-videos, bots, and, text messages with restricted numbers of words. Technology lets us choose or form new communities of like-minded others at any and all times isolating us from those who may think, look, and act differently. This means that a lot of what we know is what we already know, and comes from people who know about what we care about. It is world of continuous positive reinforcement. We want to be open-minded but wind up in segregated online communities, talking to ourselves, preaching to the choir. When we do step outside of our virtual communities, we find that others may say things we do not like.

We must keep in mind that connectivity is not just for people. Devices are connected to devices that are connected to machines, servers, and clouds. Systems mate with systems across geography and time. Communications between humans and machines are important, but there is an entire world of communications between machines (including robots and other technologies) to which we are not privy. These machines are not speaking to us. We are not plugged into their conversations. They use their own programming languages and algorithms.

> "'Connectivity is moving toward more Ethernet, wireless, and open-platform communications,' says Greg Gernert, business manager for Logix controllers at Rockwell Automation. 'Open platforms are connecting different systems that share data. This is important to move the data into the processor and

up to the MES [manufacturing execution system] and ERP [enterprise resource planning] systems. Then you have that data across the enterprise.'"[55]

Brands and organizations have opportunities to satisfy both the need to connect and the need to be disconnected. The hospitality industry is doing this already. Want to get away from the world while connecting with your family? There are many options. You can have a multi-generational spa holiday or resort vacation at a very isolated place or in your own time-share home. Airbnb allows individuals to connect to a different culture, foreign neighborhood, or an American community. You may be alone but you are connected to some place.

Delay and Desire

This paradox has guided the luxury couture industry for decades. Fashion events showcase designers' collections twice a year, and then, a buyer, filled with desire to own and wear the gown or suit must wait as it is sewn for her. Or, that Birkin bag which is lustfully coveted for its style and caché, comes with an excruciating waiting list. If you wish to pre-order a pair of Manolo Blanik shoes, go ahead, but you will have to wait to slip it onto your foot. Couture is built on the concept of wanting and waiting.

This tension between immediacy and waiting is exacerbated by the fact that today we can have our needs met instantly. Why wait? Waiting seems antiquated and antediluvian. Same day service is available across many categories. Internet shopping makes instantly obtaining goods easy. We exist in a world of real time. Real time is now: we have no patience for waiting. We live in the moment because with real time, we live from now to now. And yet, waiting, as the luxury goods purveyors know, heightens the desire. The anticipation of seeing your name move up the list requires patience and is titillating. It may be agonizing but the reward is glorious.

However, it is difficult to resist the desire for immediacy in our brave new world. Some fashion houses are changing their approach to delay by offering their collections immediately after the shows. This has created a disturbance within the business. There is disagreement about the value and inherent nature of waiting. On the one hand, there are brands that are laser-focused on the consumer who wants speedy availability of the item as well as modern (mass produced, more high tech/digital) production.

A good example is the tie-up of Nike and Givenchy with the clothing line created by Givenchy's designer, Riccardo Tisci. Mr. Tisci believes the time has come to disrupt the fashion industry.

> "'I think fashion has to modernize,' he says. 'In the past two decades, we've been stuck on the same way to produce, to present. These new changes are very important: fewer seasons, individuality, buy-now-wear-now. I think people want the clothes right away. We need a new way to deliver and present. It's time.'"[56]

On the other hand, there are couturiers, such as Karl Lagerfeld who see time as essential to luxury. After all, time means crafting, creating, customizing. "'It's a mess.' Karl Lagerfeld's verdict on the high-speed economy that has lately taken hold of the luxury industry is succinct.' '… The reality is you have to give people time to make their choice, to order the clothes or handbags, and to produce them beautifully, so that editors can photograph them. This way is chaos.'"[57] François-Henri Pinault, CEO of Kering group, (Gucci, Brioni and Bottega Veneta), praised, "the allure of 'anticipation' and the value of building desire in a consumer."[58] As with food, it is a choice between fast (food, fashion) or slow (food, fashion).

Is there some way to maximize both? Can there be a brand that creates anticipation and delivers instantly? Does anticipation need to be over many days, or can it be created over one day? Recently, the shoe designer, Freda Salvador sent an email to customers announcing a sample sale. The email, which stated, "the countdown begins now" indicated that the sale would begin at 6AM Pacific Time, the next day. Customers had a 24-hour window for waiting. Ms. Salvador's hip, crafted shoes come in a few styles, and tend to sell out quickly. There are only two physical stores, both in California. The anticipation, created in just 24-hours, for the sample sale was so great that, once it began, in mere minutes the website crashed. The crash was so intense that it took another 24 hours to reboot. As an apology for the crash, Freda Salvador offered a 30 percent discount on full price shoes as well as the continuation of the sample sale.[59] The Internet allows the maximization of desire and delay if brands take advantage of the opportunities.

Tesla started taking orders for the Model 3, the lower priced vehicle (starting at US$35,000) in April 2016. For a US$1000 deposit, a prospective owner could find a place on the wait list, which was expected to be at least two years. In interviews with "wait-listers," it turns out that people will wait for this highly desired vehicle that will begin production at the end of 2017. Prospective buyers are so desirous of the vehicle that they are committing to the vehicle purchase sight unseen. However, to address the long wait and the anticipation, while increasing the desire, Tesla announced in August 2016 that a "wait-lister" could lease a Tesla Model S Sedan or a Tesla Model X crossover for the two-year period for reduced fees of US$593/month for the Model S Sedan and US$730/month for the Tesla Model X.[60]

Research on online grocery shopping indicates that people ordering online foods and beverages purchase "better-for-you" items than when they shop in the physical grocery store. When in the physical store, shoppers give in to the impulse; people concede to the immediate gratification. But, when shopping online, people choose "relatively fewer vices" because they are not faced with the urge of desire. The researchers provide several reasons for the healthier choices online, such as seeing a "representation" of the item rather than physically holding the item. The desire is diminished by not being in the store, and because of the knowledge that there will be wait-time for the delivery.[61]

Desire and delay are built into the couture brand's experience. Other brands have to determine whether their experiences include instantaneous and immediate, or whether their customers can handle a degree of anticipation. Desire and delay are needs that are bigger than the purchase cycle: these are contradictory needs that must be addressed in the creating and delivering of the total brand experience.

TIMELINESS AND TIMELESSNESS

Related to **Delay and Desire,** this is the unique paradox of the desire for innovation/novelty *and* the need for things that have stood the tests of time: the latest and the legacy, old and new. Technology has accelerated the pace of new products and services. We are used to replacing phones, laptops, and other digital, smart, mobile devices, and connected appliances with new versions on a regular basis. We fear missing the immediate ownership of the latest and the greatest. People around the world will wait on line, overnight, regardless of weather just to buy the newest Apple device.

And, yet, at the same time, we seek the authenticity, heritage, customs and legacies of products and service steeped in tradition. Etsy, the online craft forum, is a paean to crocheted medallion quilts, handmade dangling earrings, knitted Argyle socks, and all sorts of imaginative, high quality craftsmanship. Vintage clothing stores sell authentic outfits from our parents' and grandparents' decades. The Cadillac brand website states that its interiors are "crafted to pair the beautiful with the technical. In the XT5, refined woods, leathers and trims have been chosen with care to complement its forward-thinking features."[62]

Levi's invented blue jeans. It has an amazing heritage. On its website, the brand confirms its history *and* its modernity, by being both old and new. The statement is that Levi's® Made & Crafted®

builds on the legacy of 140 years "by designing tomorrow's classics using today's best materials and construction techniques."[63]

GQ magazine ran a story in March 2016 called, "The New Classic Cars, Are Younger than You Think." The *GQ* editors identified vehicles that may be considered masterworks. An interesting idea in the article is that cars that may only be 20 years old but are now instant classics.[64]

Additionally, as we press onward at warp speeds, we find ourselves wanting the time to slow down. As we continuously click in real time, we long for the time to cut loose for rest and relaxation.

In this new Paradox Planet, time, an intangible, has become one of our most precious resources. Think about the language we use in referring to time: it is so similar to how we speak about money. We say: save time, waste time, spend time, time management, lose time, out of time, time deposits, time deficits, time limits, etc. Time is a currency that we use to calibrate our days, but it is also flow of energy (remember, time flies) that keeps us going. When Benjamin Franklin said, "Time is money," he could have also said that time is the current tide that propels us forward.

Simon Garfield says in *The Daily Telegraph*, that technology had altered our relationship with time in significant ways. He points out that while we despair at the thought of gradualness and deceleration, we participate in the slow food movement; artisanal, handmade products, foodstuffs and beverages; we covet the resort and spa vacation where we can be cut off from civilization; and we knit our hearts out to make our lives cozy and warm enough for the Hygge to envelope us.[65] Hygge is a Danish word that means a special feeling of coziness and comfort associated with a feeling of relaxation and contentment. In fact, *The New York Times Book Review* devoted its "Help Desk/ How-To and Self-Help" page to Hygge books with the title: "Getting Hygge with it: tips on how to relax, cuddle, sip cocoa, bake pastries, knit sweaters and above all – drink coffee."[66]

Roberto Ferdman writes that the desire for "now" has affected the consumption of tea in the United Kingdom, and, the demise of the teatime concept. Apparently, tea is not in sync with the accelerated pace of our lives. It is perceived as dreary, tediously traditional, and unexciting. "Many people these days do not want to take the time to brew tea, and even fewer will interrupt their busy days for the leisurely, civilized ritual of afternoon tea, a 19th-century invention of Anna, seventh Duchess of Bedford, who decided that tea and cakes were the best antidote to a late afternoon "sinking feeling." Coffee appears to be the drink of choice for the younger generations, most particularly because it is "way more cool" and seriously caffeinated.[67] If we are going to slow down for anything, at least make it something that keeps me moving faster. Today, we can avoid the seventh Duchess of Bedford's sinking feeling by tapping an app. Why stop to contemplate when you can instantly find an antidote for whatever ails you?

Part of the paradox of old and new is the current nostalgia affecting concert events. The hallowed Carnegie Hall in New York City is featuring a Sixties cultural event in 2017, as this is the fiftieth anniversary of The Summer of Love with its iconic fashion and design. There will be a fiftieth anniversary concert at Monterey, CA, celebrating the original 1967 Monterey Pop music festival that brought Jimi Hendrix and Janis Joplin to a wider audience.

In a discussion of fashion and art nostalgia, Sadie Stein writes that, "As the deep vaults of history are made accessible to everyone via technology, the past has become an alternative present." She describes how swiping Instagram reveals people who "dress up like flappers, cook like Victorians, or decorate their homes as if they were goat herders in 17th Century Lithuania." Today's nostalgia is Utopian in what some say is our current Dystopian environment. "Right now, technology affords us the ability to dress in one decade, eat in another and enjoy music of a third, without abandoning the comforts of now."[68] It is interesting that nostalgia was originally a word for homesickness; referring to the pain of aching for home, not the pleasure of authentically recreating past eras. We seem to crave authenticity in a world of shrinking truths.

Brands have an opportunity to capitalize on the conflicting needs of being in the "now" with authenticity from past decades. In the liquor category, Jim Beam and Jack Daniels are establishing their heritage credibility for a modern group of drinkers. KFC is currently making a remarkable comeback by focusing on their traditional, iconic mealtime buckets of chicken. The familiar, timeless Colonel, and his values are back, but in a timely, humorous, contemporary manner. There is something compelling about revisiting a relevant, repackaged icon right now.

In a nod to this paradox, *Financial Times* ran a fashion article, with the title, "Enter the now age: In Los Angeles, hippie crystals are being repolished and repackaged as the most chic of talismans." The writer quotes from a book by Ruby Warrington called, *Material Girl, Mystical World: The Now Age Guide to a High Vibe Life*. As *Financial Times* points out, crystals are a "resurgent" idiosyncrasy from the past that are enrapturing Now Age Millennials.[69]

Old is new is very apparent in the food and restaurant industry. Recently, *The New York Times* reported that the "The Hippies Have Won" since our current food must-haves are actually staples of the Sixties and early Seventies. Supermarket shelves and chill-cases are filled with ingredients and staples from the tie-dyed, granola-eating, flower power, counterculture. Soy milk, almond milk, Kombucha, kelp, daikon, nori, and tofu are no longer strange. Vegetarians, vegans and macrobiotic dieters are everywhere. Writing about this modern food awakening, Christine Muhlke says:

> "Co-op staples of that time — the miso, tahini, dates, seeds, turmeric and ginger that were absorbed from other cultures and populated the Moosewood restaurant cookbooks — now make appearances at some of the most innovative restaurants in the country, where menus are built around vegetables and heritage grains. Vegetarianism and veganism are on the rise; and kale, the bacon of the clean-eating moment, is now routinely heaped on salad plates across the land."[70]

Abundant and Rare

The French branding expert, Jean-Noël Kapferer, writes extensively about luxury. He examines the traditional concept of luxury as something exclusive and rare. A luxury brand in its classic sense is "an inessential, desirable item that is expensive or difficult to obtain."[71] In his writings, and in a seminal article, he describes a new concept of luxury that brand owners might consider: luxury can be both widely available *and* exclusive: he calls it "abundant rarity."[72] His concept is based on the discussion of how a luxury brand can remain a luxury brand if it is so available that it is no longer exclusive.

This is a paradoxical conundrum. If a brand remains highly exclusive with limited production units and waiting lists, it is a smaller, coveted brand than if it had wide distribution. But, to satisfy the desires of people around the globe, some luxury brands are not difficult to obtain. One no longer has to travel to Paris to find Louis Vuitton, Chanel, or Hermes. Once a luxury brand is widely available it becomes less exclusive, even if it maintains its price premium. It may run the risk of losing its hard-won cachet.

Mr. Kapferer says that some luxury brands will have to figure out how to maintain the high-class aura while being available to many. As Lydia DePillis put it in an article on *washingtonpost.com*, "How can you sell enough on a quarterly basis to make Wall Street happy while at the same time maintaining the aura of exclusivity that got you where you were in the first place?"[73]

Ms. DePillis is not alone in questioning the ability of a luxury brand to stay exclusive while being everywhere. There are those who do not believe that *luxury* can be both restricted and available. These experts believe that too much exposure saps luxury out of a product or service. Ms. DePillis uses Coach as an example of a brand that tried to grow, and harmed the exclusivity of the brand[74] before finding its way again.

A brief review across sources detailing Coach's history of short-term financial engineering, greater ubiquity, and the opening of discount stores, demonstrates the pitfalls that a luxury brand may face in becoming more available. Tim Hanson of *Motley Fool* said, "If you're a luxury brand with outlet stores, maybe you're not a luxury brand."[75] Since its dark period, Coach has addressed the tension of ubiquity and exclusivity, and has stepped back from the actions that changed the brand's image. It has managed to revitalize its high-end aura while remaining affordable.

Sonja Prokopec, a marketing professor and head of the LVMH-ESSEC Chair at ESSEC Business School, wrote about the "fine line" a luxury brand must walk when maximizing rarity and availability. She posits that there is an ongoing "democratization" of luxury based on elite brands going after a wider audience using creative approaches that may be blurring the line between mass and class.[76]

Some luxury brands wishing to attract more customers use strategies of brand extensions, entry-level items, and licensing. (When it comes to licensing, it is possible to take it to extremes. The luxury brand that licensed itself to demise is considered to be Pierre Cardin.) Problems occur when these strategies go beyond growth generation to brand status harm. The hope is that sibling or sub-brand buyers will trade-up within the brand, buying the iconic items.

Levels or tiers of brand offerings are one way that brands can maximize the needs of rarity and abundance. By having a high-end premium offering, and a more affordable, more available offering, Johnnie Walker Scotch created an aspirational brand. The tiers of Red, Black, Double Black, Green, and Blue Gentleman's Wager, allow consumers to enter its luxury spectrum at their own pace.[77]

American Express, which entered the credit card market as a more "high-end" card relative to Visa and MasterCard, uses a similar strategy as Johnnie Walker. The original Green card now has siblings in Gold, Platinum, and Black Centurion, not counting its entries in business cards and cards that allow you to pay off less than the actual amount. Interestingly, the Black Centurion card addresses a luxury paradox of extraordinary singular, personal status *and* belonging to a small, very elite group.

Automotive brands provide a line of vehicles from a "starter version" to a more exclusive version. These models are differentiated by price, add-ons, and badge/name. An example that works is Toyota and Lexus. The highest-end Toyota is practically the same as the low-end Lexus. Both brands have well-thought-out brand experiences. Rebranding a Ford with a new grille as a higher-priced Mercury did not work, however.

The fashion industry has managed to create different lines to protect the ultimate luxury offering. Giorgio Armani created the A/X brand for younger customers who may not have the budget for couture but want to experience Armani. The Giorgio Armani line is designed for older, wealthier women who appreciate his tailored yet high-style European look. And, Giorgio Armani Privé is for that small clientele who prefer couture rather than ready-to-wear. Armani also sells Armani Jeans and Armani Junior.

Exclusive and Affordable

An interesting twist on the paradox of abundant and rare is **Exclusive and Affordable.** In this paradox, inexpensive items are sought after because they are so hard to find. You can afford these if only you could find them.

Some brands use recurring limited time options (LTOs) to generate excitement about an affordable product such as the McRib at McDonald's or the Lava Sauce at Taco Bell. Chanel offers limited edition nail enamels each season: spring, summer, autumn, and winter. When the bottles sell out, the "season" is over.[78]

Craft beer is a category where small batches are made and coveted. Many of these beer productions sell out quickly and become highly sought after but hard to find. *Bring on The Beer* is a craft beer online site that calls itself The Pacific Northwest's #1 Craft Beer Store where you can find those "rare, deeply flavored beers that are nearly impossible to find in most states across the US." The site allows a customer to sign up for information on when small batch beers will be available and possibly be first to buy that favorite taste.[79]

The New York Times described a situation where beer fanatics will wait on line for hours just to buy the latest production of a hard to find product.

> "Modern Times Beer in San Diego and Threes Brewing in Brooklyn presell cans online and provide pickup windows for the beer. Maine Beer Company and Hoof Hearted Brewing in Marengo, Ohio, sell advance tickets to limit crowds. 'There were a couple times where we thought we'd have a riot,' said Trevor Williams, the brewer and an owner of Hoof Hearted."[80]

Esther Mobley wrote in *The San Francisco Chronicle* that some oenophiles in California now seek wines that are inexpensive but hard to find because only a small number of cases are produced. She describes a situation where wine-seekers are introduced to these wines at a restaurant, and, then, spend a lot of time online attempting to find these "Rare but Not Elite" bottles.[81]

Having different brands can isolate the most exclusive brand from the possibility of losing class for mass accessibility. Or, the decision can be made to provide a luxurious experience that is accessible. Of course, the business model is critical but the total brand experience must be clear, understandable, and valuable.

Building exclusivity into the brand experience does not mean that the brand will be expensive. Missoni sold items at Target and they sold out immediately. The original, available at Target, Alessi teakettle was a highly sought-after item. It is all about how the brand is designed and managed.

A recent article in *The Economist* told the story of Howard Johnson's (HoJo's), and how the very last restaurant is up for sale. The article traces the arc of HoJo's success starting in 1925 as an ice cream store near Boston. Those old enough to remember the 1950s become misty thinking about Howard Johnson's restaurants which were ubiquitous as places to stop and have a very good, high quality meal for the whole family: the restaurants were the "road stop" for the family vacation on President Eisenhower's new Interstate highways system. HoJo's made fried clams nationally acceptable. In the 1960s, Chefs from Le Pavillion in New York City enhanced Howard Johnson's success, as did the waitresses wearing Dior-designed uniforms. As *The Economist* points out, "A Howard Johnson's meal was 'affordable glamour' for the growing middle class."[82] In 1960, founder Howard Johnson stepped down, and his son took over the business. Pursuing a cost-cutting strategy, the business went public in 1961. Shareholders urged deeper cuts. Over the next ten years, the business was bought and sold many times, and the motor lodge division was spun off as a separate enterprise (sold to Wyndham Hotels). The rise of fast food restaurants put a final nail in the coffin.[83]

Personalization (automated) and Personal (human)

As we discussed earlier, personalization is a powerful force affecting everything we do. With technology and algorithms, it seems that anything can be personalized just when you want it, just for you. When you look up a brand online, and then go to *The New York Times* website to read the news, there will be an ad for that just-looked-at brand. Amazon will create reading lists, music suggestions, and product offerings based on what you have previously bought.

Hotels use information from their databases on your previous stays, and your loyalty club inputs, to recognize and reward you on arrival. This remembrance provides a sense of respect and status. You may receive your favorite room with your preferred soft drinks in the minibar, and your requested newspapers at your door the next morning. You are also recognized and spoken to using your name. There may be a welcome note in your room. The reams of data allow for personalization in ways that enhance your stay.

These "personal" messages are created just for each of us, but these do not provide the personal, human touch. This is why Discover Card lets you know that when you call, there will be a real person answering the phone to deal with your issue.

Recently, the decision to be completely automated has evolved with human relationships added to the mix. There is a growing category of banking and investing managed by automation. The belief is that Millennials prefer a different bank approach than their parents, and from Generation X (the cohort preceding Millennials). One of the popular "fintech" companies is SoFi. Originally designed to help Millennials with their student loans, the operation has evolved. It is aiming to become a financial center for its approximately 230,000 Henry (High Earner Not Rich Yet) customers. Although a digital play, the enterprise has sought to generate loyalty through non-digital means such as get-togethers and other events, bringing an actual human-social dimension to the robotic product.[84] Additionally, SoFi is acquiring a mobile banking app enterprise (Zenbanx) that will allow SoFi to add "conversational banking" to their experience.[85]

Geoff Colvin wrote about the insurance company USAA in the July 1, 2016 issue of *Fortune*. He described what happened when the stock markets plummeted: USAA managers in the investment area found that customers were calling rather than dealing with the company online. Although all the necessary information was available on the website, customers wanted to speak to a human being. This is one of the workplace paradoxes with which businesses must now deal: what should be automated and what should remain human? Robotics, digitization, and, algorithms can make predictions but, as of now, these cannot provide judgment. Mr. Colvin also raises this interesting dilemma. It is the trade-off decision about which we wrote earlier. Do we want efficiency across the board or do we want the best of automation and human? Not every situation is predictable or quantifiable. Many decisions are laced with visceral, instinctive, possibly unpredictable emotion. When faced with these sorts of emotional decisions, people may want to speak to, and interact with a human. As Mr. Colvin reminds us, at the moment, data, and machines do not speak or decide; people do. And, "just because technology can do a job brilliantly does not mean that it should."[86]

The concept of personalization is changing due to automation. Personalization is now "an engine" that knows you and communicates in a "personal" manner. The "personalization engine" is usually correct, and, sometimes, automated personalization is better than the human kind. The customer representative at Amazon's customer care center had the correct script, and the energetic personality to deal with a botched delivery. However, the script did not remind the customer representative that the world is round. In eagerness to solve the problem, the Amazon representative called the United States Postal Service to confirm a new delivery date. On the east coast of the United States, it was 6:15 AM. The representative reported back to the customer that the delivery service was closed today. The customer had to remind the representative that the United States Postal Service was not yet open even though it was afternoon at the customer call center. Savvy customers know that providing confusing or partial answers to the automaton on the other end of the phone is the easiest way to be connected to a real, live human being representative. However, there is that trade-off: the automaton may be programmed to know there are time zones even if it cannot be empathetic.

The maximization of the need for automated and human personalization is happening in the world of personal assistants from Apple (Siri), Amazon (Alexa), Microsoft (Cortana), and Google (Google Now). In the competition to become the preferred personal assistant, these products continuously learn from their dealings with us. According to feedback from the January CES (Consumer Electronic Show) in Las Vegas,

> "... The digital assistant's artificial intelligence capabilities will expand to handle more interactions, allowing live agents to focus their time and talent on high-value customers and more complex or critical issues."[87]

The integration of automation and humanity is a top of mind issue for which brands are creating solutions daily. It is a paradox that demands flexibility. It seems as if every day there are two or more stories about the presence of AI in our lives, for the good or the scary. It is truly good to have robots and prosthetics that work using a person's brain waves. It is good to know that algorithms still cannot create music like the Beatles or Hayden. But, it is scary to think that we are unwittingly creating our own demise, and perhaps may be replicated. Two recent articles by John Thornhill in *Financial Times* ("Artificial intelligence is running wild while humans dither" and "Don't kid yourself that robots are colleagues")[88] should give us pause that perhaps we are allowing the artificial intelligence to manage our own.

Corporate and brand strategists and scenario planners have their work cut out for them. Our changing world is getting younger and older at the same time. A brand may have customers that are Baby Boomers and Millennials. These cohorts may want the automated/human Paradox Promise delivered differently. Some brands may decide to cater to only one cohort as a target audience. But for some brands, such as hotels or the automotive industry, brands needs to have strategies, executions, and communications that satisfy both cohorts without harming the integrity of the brand's total brand experience.

Privacy and Personalization

Related to the previous paradox of optimizing automation with the humans, is the dark side of personalization: the diminishment and dissolution of privacy. We also think about it as the paradox of **Preserving Anonymity and Wanting to Be Known**. We give our personal information away while we see privacy as an eroding asset. We want the benefits of being known while we worry about the consequences. We know our data is collected but we have concerns about who is using it and how it is being used. We avoid thinking about the fact that our E-ZPass® or SunPass (transponder toll payment systems) are tracking our whereabouts as we cruise through the tollbooths. Enter the New York State Thruway at Exit 17, and hop off at Exit 24 in under 1½-hours, and you will receive a speeding ticket in the mail.

Privacy and Personalization is an ongoing debate, and affects government and other institutions not just brands and businesses. And, it is an internal debate that consumers have with themselves: how much do I say about me *and* to whom (ultimately) am I giving my information? There is a contingent, albeit small, who reject giving information. *The New York Times* called them, "the Un-Googleables, the online elusive ones." This group is "distressed about privacy, exhibitionism and other occupational hazards of social media creating a select few holdouts of the tech-savvy age."[89]

The desire for more and more personalization means that people provide more and more personal information. But this creates a privacy conundrum. Research indicates that people do weigh the costs of personalization (i.e., the loss of privacy) relative to the benefits.[90] In an odd, but maybe understandable twist, people are more concerned about others (strangers, office mates, fellow travelers, cashiers, etc.) knowing things about them than they are with big corporations knowing things. A Brookings Institution paper suggests that our understanding of privacy is not what we think, as we will behave secretly when buying personal products (condoms, for example) or reading material, but willingly hand over personal information to large enterprises that will provide convenience, speed and/or price advantages. It is called The Privacy Paradox.[91]

The role of trust is essential in the maximization of personalization and privacy. The degree of trust a person has that their information will be handled with the utmost security affects the assessment of risk to privacy. (See the later explanation of The Trustworthy Brand Value™ equation, in Part 4.) Do we trust who or what is happening to our in-home conversations while our Echo or Cortana listen? Do we care that our Vizio TV is uploading and distributing our personal data without our permission?

Consumers are aware of the personalization-privacy paradox but do not self-blame for providing their personal information. They expect the companies with which they do business to be more vigilant. Consumers seem to recognize that there are risks but they appear willing to accept the risks up to a point. According to a recent study by Gemalto, a digital security company, only 30 percent of consumers believe companies are taking their personal data protection very seriously; 58 percent of consumers fear they will be victims of an online data breach; and, 66 percent would be unlikely to do business with organizations responsible for exposing financial and sensitive information. The study reflects the opinions of 9000 people worldwide.[92]

Although we provide our data willingly, we draw the line when it comes to our children, even though we have no qualms about posting family pictures on Facebook and other social sites. Some parents have made their families famous online. The brouhaha over the Hello Barbie products that track the child's behavior, then, uploading it to the cloud was just one event in what is now a larger unhappiness with the reality of digital playthings. Many new "tech-laden" toys capture an infant's or a child's speech and actions. Vtech, a company that makes technologically enhanced toys was hacked, and according to *techdirt,* an online site, "the names, email addresses, passwords, and home addresses of 4,833,678 parents, and the first names, genders, and birthdays of more than 200,000 kids" were taken.[93] More recently, CloudPets™ (sweet-looking, cuddly, smiling stuffed animals that are cloud-connected) experienced a data breach exposing over 2 million kids and parents.[94] And, in Germany, the governmental telecommunications oversight group issued a "destroy" warning to parents of children owning an Internet-enabled doll named Cayla. Apparently, the doll has a system that can be connected to anyone within thirty feet. Since a child's conversations with the doll could be listened to, the doll is deemed a spy. According to the article in *The Wall Street Journal,* there is a €25,000 fine and two years in prison for those not "executing" the spy-doll.[95]

We provide data willingly. But, data are also collected when we have not provided permission. Our smartphones deliver data. Our smart appliances provide data. Our televisions. Every search provides data. As we move quickly towards the Internet of Things, we need to have something more than promises of security. Our cars provide data. As the automotive companies face a future where the idea of transportation will be different from today, they are increasingly looking at artificial intelligence tie-ups that will enhance moving people from point A to point B without a owning a car. At the same time, the cars are becoming packed with technologies that are vulnerable to hackers. *Financial Times* reported that Uber is moving towards becoming a data collector by "personalizing" its app. According to the article, Uber will use its app to predict where users will go at certain times, and will suggest places to go based on past trips with drop-off and pick-up locations.[96] Would we stop using Uber knowing that it will be probing into our lives? The latest news indicates that when we go to the mall, we are followed via our mobile phones' "locate me" function.[97] Are we aware that the shopping mall tracks our in-mall behaviors while using corresponding social media and email correspondence to send us messages with promotions or product/service information? Would we stop shopping at the mall? Shopping on Amazon does not mean our personal data are not collected.

Not only do we live in a world that is always on, we live in a world where we are always monitored. There is a worry that we are not significantly proactive when it comes to protecting our waking and sleeping moments. There are discussions about the effect of constant surveillance on our behaviors and attitudes. For example, if we are always being watched, will we be as open and creative?[98] What type of society will we have when we are known so well? And, it is not just the tracking of our actions, feelings, and speech: our data are analyzed and interpreted; our data are so useful that our data are sold.

The more connected we become, the more difficult it is for us to feel secure about privacy. In our current environment, Greta Garbo's request, "I want to be alone" would not only be ignored but be impossible. Only a complete off-the-grid disconnection from digital, mobile, satellite, and drone technology would begin to alleviate the fear of privacy loss. Not only is that an extreme position to take, we have already committed more than enough information already. This is one of the paradoxes that must be solved. We have already donated more information than we could possibly imagine. How this information is managed relative to the benefits of respect, recognition, status and appreciation is a massive opportunity.

This privacy-personalization tension is a paradox that brands and enterprises must actively manage. Brands and enterprises must be transparent in how they manage personal information, and understand the line between personalization and peeping. Peeping is creepy. Using information from a customer's Facebook page or LinkedIn entry to personalize a service is a benefit to some but may be going too far for others.

TECHNOLOGICAL CONTROL AND HUMAN CONTROL

Different from **Personalization (automated) and Personal (human)**, this paradox is about decision-making. Now that more and more of our products and services are automated, in many instances, our ability to control things and events is ceded to a machine. It means that our decisions are allocated to robots rather than to our reasoning.

Financial investment is an activity that people believe should be made with objectivity rather than emotion: a perfect job for a robot. As we mentioned, algorithms appear to make better predictions. The question is about what decisions do we take based on the predictions? Who makes those decisions? Shouldn't judgment be involved in making a decision?

As reported in *Financial Times*, "the greatest danger lies not in heeding a robo-advisor but behaving like an emotional human being." The article explained that a computer could provide more sophisticated advice than a stockbroker; the robots are user-friendly and fast. "A computer with access to a standard array of index funds and exchange-traded funds can devise a suitable long-term investment strategy for most people in a blink."[99]

However, there is a new, "retro" move toward adding human help to the array of computerized financial services. How one invests is serious, complex, and, emotional. Digitized checklists and descriptions of products along with algorithms and automation cannot provide the answers to the more opaque, nuanced, and, sensitive questions. There are reasons major investment banks and wealth management groups have humans on board.

Cars represent another area where there is a lot of action regarding robotic decision-making. Autonomous vehicles are being developed as we write, with some autonomous-element-vehicles already on the road. Although catching the imagination of many young people, there is a view that robotic vehicles will be of most benefit to senior citizens who have lost their ability to drive well or at all. The growing 65-year old and older population of Baby Boomers grew up with cars: cars were part of the move into adulthood. Now, they want to drive but find themselves losing their peripheral vision, motor skills, confidence and edge. *Bloomberg BusinessWeek* reported that Ford Motor Company sees autonomous vehicles as a strategic approach to address the needs of the United States' aging population. However, *Bloomberg* reported, "The focus is shifting from a car or a robot that can move around by itself to people having the ability to decide for themselves where they want to move, when they want to move."[100] The managing editor of *The Greenwood Commonwealth* in Mississippi wrote that the race is on to make autonomous driving a norm by 2025. Tesla already has an autonomous option, and Uber has autonomous vehicles in a Pittsburgh, Pennsylvania test,[101] which has recently faced some challenges. And, as we learn, Intel, the company that taught us to look for its computer chip inside of the computer is now putting money into chips that run autonomous vehicles.

The paradox of *who or what* is in control is prevalent in medicine. Robotics is changing how surgery is performed. The question is: do we trust non-human systems to be making life and death decisions?

Beating players in Jeopardy, Go, or chess is one thing. Autonomous vehicles are not a far-out concept because already we use trains that are driverless at airports to go to the rental car area at SFO; to get around to the different gates at DFW; or to go through Customs and Immigration at MIA. In the military, we accept drone warfare, but people are directing the machines.

"Non-human-in-charge" is changing medicine. For example, United States researchers developed the world's first surgical robot that, reports say,

> "... Outperforms human surgeons when operating autonomously in certain surgeries, paving the way for clinical trials. For now, the robot known as STAR takes a bit longer (than a surgeon), and it is a tool rather than a truly autonomous agent."[102]

Another example is the Sedasys sedation machine, created by Johnson & Johnson, to automate the sedation of patients undergoing colon-cancer screenings. The machine was designed to improve care, and, of course, reduce costs. Rather than employ the anesthesiologist, Sedasys would do the common sedation procedure more efficiently, and, hopefully, more effectively. However, the machine was pulled from the marketplace after angry responses from anesthesiologists who believe that Sedasys was a safety hazard, and not a better choice than humans.[103]

The Wall Street Journal reported that scientists are working on an algorithm that will recognize whether that bump on your skin is a cancerous lesion. The idea is to use artificial intelligence to screen for skin cancer using medical images and normal photographs. As the journalist asked, "Will your phone be able to recognize melanoma?"[104] Maybe it can. But, would you trust your mobile phone to make such a decision?

Trust plays an important role in optimizing paradox promises. Where do we wish to place our trust? In what do we wish to place our trust? A brand's promise is affected by trust, as it is a multiplier of the customer's perceived value. Since people prefer to not make a trade-off decision, there has to be a way that human control and technological control are maximized in a most trustworthy manner.

Right now, the trust scales seem to be tipping towards robotic control. But the issue remains critical: can trust be digitized? How far are we willing to go in ceding control? Can we feel as safe and sound when trust is placed in artificial intelligence? Are we living in a Phillip Dick story?

In March 2016, a New Zealand conference of engineers, military personnel, and scientists reported that people tend to "over trust" robots even when the robot has made a mistake. Even "when it is clear that there is a serious malfunction," people will still relinquish their own control to the robot.[105] We tend to assign human emotions and values to robots even though these are not able to be (as of yet) empathetic. (Have you ever lost your temper with your GPS system when she tells you your destination is on the left and it is not?) We consider that robots will not only make the right decision for us, but also make the moral decision for us. We know the robots do not have souls but we are willing to cede control on these important life and death issues.

In episode #21 of the first (1967) season of *Star Trek*, "The Return of the Archons" (recently aired on BBC channel cable TV), an Earth-like society on planet Beta III has been ruled by an elusive leader, Landru. The people on the planet are robotic and emotionless, with no self-expression. It turns out that Captain Kirk and Dr. Spock determine that there is no real leader: the now deceased leader programmed a computer to rule the population. The computer, as Captain Kirk points out, has no soul, and, therefore, has not allowed creativity and free self-expression. Although these original episodes have been analyzed many times, the closing scenes with Captain Kirk arguing with the computer program about being soul-less is relevant to our situation today where we, sometimes unquestioningly, put ourselves in the hands of robots and artificial intelligence, delegating our decisions rather than creatively figuring out what is best.

The WEF focused on the underlying ethical dilemmas posed by artificial intelligence in a 2015 report unveiled at Davos. "Whether or not we are comfortable with AI may already be moot," the report says. "More pertinent questions might be whether we can and ought to build trust in systems that can make decisions beyond human oversight that may have irreversible consequences." Although the report recognized the enormous benefits of AI, it also expressed concern (fear) about a malevolent form of intelligence that might not work in concert of our best interests.[106]

Clearly, we have given over our ability to meet someone special to algorithms, and swipes, at eHarmony, match.com and Tinder. Why count reps or steps during your exercise routine when the fitness band or app can keep you on track? We no longer have to think about turning the thermostat up or down when Nest can manage that task for us. Emotions need not be written when along with liking, Facebook now has Love, Haha, Wow, Sad, and Angry. ATM maker, Diebold, believes that using smart technology, the "ATM experience" will soon be "a more breezy, personal experience that does away with debit cards. With high security, the machines will be able to scan eyes and communicate with your smart phone."[107] We see that robotic animals help comfort the elderly, such as Hasbro's "Joy for All" kitty cat. We fly on Airbus airplanes where human workers direct robots that drill in all the screws responsible for holding the plane together.[108]

However, it is important to understand the problems people have before developing, embedding or applying a technology. A decade ago, we worked with a client that developed a technology allowing you to turn on your oven from your office or workplace when you were running late. Instead of coming home to begin supper, you could start your meal from your desk chair. After explaining how this would work using your mobile phone, over the course of 10 focus group interviews in London, all respondents indicated that if they were running late they would buy take-away food on the way home rather than turn on the oven to cook. They wanted new appliances that warmed rather than cooked.

One of the aspects of invisible technologies that decide for us is the shift in accountability. If something goes amiss, we can always blame the machine. When we maximize technological control and human control, hopefully we can maintain some of our responsibilities. If not, we are disconnecting from the positive or negative sides of decision-making. As Dr. Hans Moravec, Professor at the Robotics Institute of Carnegie Mellon University has said, "What is hardest for humans is easiest for machines and vice versa."

We wrote about the optimization of these two types of control in *The 2017 IHG Trends Report* as **Do It for Me in My Way and Do It For Myself**.[109] A paradoxical dimension of **Technological Control and Human Control**, this IHG Report paradox highlights that we want to do things for ourselves and we expect the machine to do it for us but in the way we want. Take something simple like making dinner. Online we join Blue Apron, Plated, Fresh Direct, or vegetable-focused Purple Carrot, Gathered Table online planner, and the takeout app, Sweetgreen.[110] These dinners are to be assembled and prepared as instructed. If you prefer to create dinner yourself, that is your decision.

Hospitality is an industry that has succeeded in maximizing **Do It for Me in My Way and Do It For Myself.** Some travelers prefer to avoid all human contact on their journeys by beginning online seeking information through booking online using OTAs, and then, using the kiosk at the airport, or using a smart phone. There is the hotel kiosk, and room key enabled on their mobile phones. Check out is the reverse. Other travelers prefer personal attention all along the way: they wish to use their travel agents, the check-in counters, a check-in desk, and a concierge. The hospitality industry has managed to provide "guest journeys" where travelers can pick and choose how much technology and how much human contact they wish to have.

Another way to look at the concept of control comes from a recent Accenture report. Essentially, it reminds us that humans are creating and designing technology that teaches the machines to think like humans. It refers to this as "human-centered technology" where we are creating the controller that will control the way we want to be controlled. The report, "Technology for People," focuses on "the emergence of technology for people, by people: technology that seamlessly anticipates our needs and delivers hyper-personalized experiences."[111] The issue is whether we can trust the people who imbue the machines with these human-like capabilities. Programmers are people and people have innate bias for the good or bad. We have to believe that the programmers are free from malevolent thoughts. Let's hope this is true.

The maximization of robotics and humanity in decision-making is a serious ethical, moral, economic, social, and, now, political issue. Organizations and brands must consider the ramifications when it comes to addressing this paradox with all of its dimensions. Each industry and category is different enough that there is no one-size-fits-all solution. Clearly, what works in the automotive industry will not work in the restaurant industry. The significance of the paradox has to be considered. This is not one of those paradoxes that will require an online, mobile digital marketing campaign. Brands and the organizations that own them will have to apply a large degree of thoughtfulness to how each optimizes in the best interest of their users and potential users.

Indulgence and Wellness

The world of food and eating food; cooking food; growing food; selling food; and processing (or not) food has undergone massive alterations. Natural, organic, unprocessed, home or locally grown, artisanal, small batch, non-GMO, gluten-free, and soy-free have surpassed the fat free, low calorie, sugar free mantras of the 1990s. The 1966 Erewhon Natural Food stores where you brought your own jars to be filled with musty, dusty, dried beans, and oil-topped natural peanut butter, where the fuzzy vegetables seemed to be weeks old with a "stepped-on" look, have been replaced by Whole Foods, a palace of perfect fruits and vegetables with a conscientious values set, and superior social consciousness to make even the most giving, righteous person feel small. Somewhere down the aisles are people who feel smart when reading the easy-to-understand labels of the "clean" foodstuffs, and yet who desire the delicious hit of extravagance that fat, sugar, and calories can bring. For those of us who shop at a Wal-Mart or Piggly Wiggly instead, we still face the same desire for healthful food and indulgent food. It is the paradox of **Indulgence and Wellness**, or **Diet and Delight**.

As asked in *Dairy Foods* magazine, a magazine reporting on dairy processing and dairy industry news, "How does a dairy processor address the public's enlightened attitude about nutrition while still appealing to its inclination toward indulgence?"[112] The idea of having a permissible pleasure is very potent even for those on restrictive diets, whether mandated or self-imposed. Interestingly, the absence of "bad" can be more powerful than the inclusion of fats, calories, and sugars. We have observed this over the past decades. Absence of "bad ingredients" is a very good approach. *Dairy Foods* calls it "the premium paradox" of frozen desserts, when someone might select the high fat, high sugar, and high caloric option rather than the low calorie, no sugar, and low fat option, which has an ingredient list of unpronounceable additives.[113]

Chipotle burritos are large and caloric but all is forgiven due to the Chipotle rigor for serving Food with Integrity: non-GMO, non-growth hormone; no artificial anything; grass-fed, happy cows and pigs; and locally grown herbs when possible. The "clean" food at Panera Bread is marketed as "food as it should be." The belief system on the Panera Bread website says, "We believe in raising, serving and eating food that is good and good for you." At the same time, this "clean food" depending on your order, can be highly caloric, filled with sodium and, it can be somewhat fat-laden. For example, the Bacon, Egg & Cheese on an Asiago Cheese Bagel has 680 calories, 1370 mg of sodium, 33 grams of fat, and 14 grams of saturated fat. The whole size Fiji Apple Salad with Chicken has 450 calories, 580 mg of sodium and 34 grams of fat. The Romaine and Kale Caesar with Chicken has 530 calories, with 1060 mg of sodium. Healthful and indulgent, the healthfulness comes from the 'cleanness' of the food while the indulgence comes from the fat and salt.[114] The good news is that information on calories, fat, salt, and so forth of these "clean" foods is readily available. We can make our own decisions about, "How much is enough?" Clean food with no bad ingredients or bad sourcing behaviors is considered a competitive advantage and can be used for bragging rights. At the moment, the CEOs of Chipotle and Panera Bread are engaged in a very public tiff about whose food is "cleaner."

Craft beers and stouts are carefully made in small batches. Some are hard to find because they have limited production and distribution. These breweries use pure, natural ingredients, avoiding the ingredients industrial brewers include. One of the best according to the Internet is "Good People El Gordo Imperial Stout," from a small brewery in Birmingham, Alabama. An 8oz bottle has 417 calories. Some beers from AB InBev contain GMO corn syrup, GMO dextrose, GMO corn or GMO rice. Miller Lite, which has fewer calories than regular beer, uses corn syrup to create taste.

In *Six Rules of Brand Revitalization, Second Edition*[115], we report on the changes that Nestlé had to make to its signature diet, frozen food brand, Lean Cuisine. The company was forced to revamp the product line as consumers turned away from frozen foods and preferred to purchase "fresh, unprocessed, healthier options with fewer and better-for-you ingredients." And, it is not just the ingredient list that hampers the "healthful" image of Lean Cuisine: in-home preparation of frozen foods, the defrosting and the reheating, tends to change the food's taste and the texture. As we discussed, Nestlé recognized that not only has frozen food lost relevance in terms of "healthfulness" but also lost relevance because the brand was using "outdated" ideas about weight loss, weight management, and weight control. "Increasingly consumers see organic, fresh, and freshly prepared foods as better weight management tools than low fat, low calorie, and tasteless varieties. Lean Cuisine is currently trying to reignite relevance with weight conscious customers through huge alterations to the range of meals, better-for-you ingredients and superior processes. Nestlé's other frozen global entries are also being changed to match customers' expectations and eating habits." Currently, the Lean Cuisine menu is replete with "indulgent" meals made with "healthful" ingredients, with options like Deep Dish Spinach and Mushroom Pizza; Philly-Style Steak and Cheese Panini; Asian Style Pot Stickers; Meatloaf with Mashed Potatoes; and Creamy Basil Chicken with Tortellini.[116]

Maximizing our desires for diet and delight is a massive opportunity: find the sweet spot between healthful/hunger/nourishment/energy satisfaction *and* pleasurable indulgence/escape/reward/treat. This paradox is not just for human foods. The Purina Dog Chow Healthy Weight brand indicates that it is, "For dogs striving to achieve an ideal weight, our Healthy Weight recipe is made with real chicken and 10% fewer calories (than Dog Chow® Complete Adult) but doesn't compromise on taste with a combination of tender chunks and crunchy kibble that dogs love."[117] We love our pets, and want to indulge them, but we also want healthy, wellness pet foods with great ingredients.

And, this paradox is not just related to the food industry. The wellness industry is a paradox of indulgence and healthful. We aim for physical and mental health through exercise classes, meditation, and vitamins. We purchase weights and equipment to use at home, or we attend fitness sessions. We take wellness vacations, and interact with workplace wellness programs. But, we also splurge on plastic surgery, aesthetician treatments, fillers, Botox®, Dysport®, massages, spa treatments, beauty salons, lotions, potions, and makeup. *The Global Wellness Institute* figures for 2015 indicate that we are indulging in wellness to the tune of $3.7 trillion, including the spa industry at $99 billion, beauty and anti-aging at $999 billion, and fitness-mind-body at $542 billion.[118]

For those who can afford it, wellness seeking can be indulged in a variety of ways. An advertisement in the February 2017 issue of *Travel and Leisure* magazine for Canyon Ranch®, the all-inclusive group of health and wellness resorts states, "Find Inner Fire, Renew your perspective."[119] The wellness options listed on the website for the Tucson, Arizona property are remarkably varied, and indulgent: more than 40 fitness classes, 4 swimming pools, an 80,000 square foot spa complex, guided hikes and walks, personalized programs, gourmet eating with healthful snacks. The prices for this wellness weekend or week could also be considered an indulgence.

The Wall Street Journal ran a story on yoga vacations where you can find serenity, relieve stress, and be, surprisingly, self-indulgent, including some prices around US $6500. The article points out that if you are not fond of yoga but want to unwind in what they call "Body and Sojourn," you can try a Wildfitness® Boot Camp in Zanzibar, Crete or Scotland; or a swimming holiday from SwimTrek®. Of the six different wellness options highlighted, the prices ranged from around US $1000 to US $5800.[120]

And, now, we can have our indulgent wellness services and products delivered to our homes. In the United Kingdom and the United States, there are now multiple apps for ordering on-demand spa, hair salon, nail salon, make-up application, and other services such as yoga and faux tans, to your home: an Uber business model for beauty services. *Financial Times* referred to this as "reinventing Avon" for the gig-economy era.[121]

Flowers add beauty to our lives, and, for some of us, having fresh flowers is a way to feel centered and calm. Flower arrangements are "meditative," and, the scents of flowers bring happiness. On the other hand, having fresh flowers is rather indulgent unless you have your own garden. Providers of daily/repeat fresh flowers are not just disrupting the floral industry but catering to the paradox of healthful and indulgent. There are currently several companies that deliver blooms to your home.[122]

The word indulgence comes from the Latin word to indulge, *indulgere*, and meaning, "to give free rein to." We all have a time when we want to let loose and eat or do something self-gratifying. But, we know that there are "costs" for indulgence: the wellness of mind and body. Consumers want brands and organizations to optimize indulgence and wellness. Consumers want to believe that your brand is a permissible pleasure, something that provides the benefits of indulgence while being allowable.

IMPROVED ME AND IMPROVED WE

In September 2016, a strategy group released a white paper that depicted a decent world, not a dark, deranged one, a world of conscientiousness not carnage. The paper focused on what the group called the *Consciousness Economy* defined as the "embrace of a collective awareness of what is good for me is good for the world." "… Actions involving commerce that directly or indirectly makes the world better…. Or at least does no harm."[123] This white paper underscores a paradox that we have previously written about,[124] and that is pursuing personal, self-improvement *while* striving for public, civic or global betterment. We desire self-satisfaction *and* selflessness. This paradox crosses age cohorts. For example, a review of Gen Z respondents (ages thirteen and fourteen) indicated, "They believe they are responsible for building a new social order. And, they are tolerant, optimistic and pragmatic about their roles and vision."[125]

Sabre Corporation also released a report on "behaviors" driving opportunities within the hospitality industry in Asia Pacific singling out "betterment." The information from Sabre indicates that while people want to improve themselves, they also want to "do good."[126]

People consider their personal, individual behaviors as well as their group behaviors within a social context that has social meaning: behaviors that are good for me *must also be* good for you, the community, and the world. How we behave as individuals and how we behave within a social context has social meaning: good for me *while* good for us. This is at the very heart of The Age of I: individual decisions and actions can influence the community's (society's) issues.

Jared Steinberg created a tour company that helps "indigenous populations preserve their land and resources." In an interview with

Diane Daniel for *The New York Times*, he said that he provides his groups with water bottles that they must refill; he uses carbon offsets for guests' flights; he brings his groups to homes of those living off the grid; and in Rwanda, he takes the group to a market where they buy their ingredients for dinner, and then, are taught how to cook a local meal. His feeling is that along with the financial contribution the guests make, they also become more aware of the issues.[127]

The idea of volunteering while vacationing has several aspects. It can be a learning experience, such as what Mr. Steinberg delivers to his tourists, or, it can be actually doing something constructive such as Carnival Cruise Line's, Fathom™ brand, for impact travel. With impact travel, cruise passengers choose from a list of volunteer activities at their destination. It maximizes the desire for personal travel that broadens my horizons and my desire to make a difference.

Improve Me and Improve We has been increasing over the past five years. Some[128] suggest that growing institutional distrust; a new definition of wellness and of wellbeing; immediate awareness both visually and vocally, through social media channels, of natural disasters; and the continual growth of online networking, are pushing people to want to make a difference in themselves, and in the world. Social media gives people a very loud voice, providing personal empowerment on issues ranging from climate change to social justice and other ethical issues. We can be good citizens locally and globally through networking. Because we have a need to belong, individuals seek through their networks, ways in which they can organize to "do good deeds." We want to be helpful while helping ourselves. And, we see prevention as a way to help: we can take personal preventive steps, managing our health, for example while building homes (Habitat for Humanity), or volunteering at a hospital. *Huffington Post* reported that in 2016, 62.6 million Americans volunteered to help others.[129]

An article about China in January 2017 reported that among young people "voluntourism" is fast becoming part of one's lifestyle. "Voluntourism", also known as volunteer tourism, combines volunteer work with travel. A global phenomenon, it is gaining momentum among young Chinese, especially college students." In 2016, a company called Ciweishixi, a company for intern opportunities based in Shenzhen, China, launched a South Asia "voluntourism" program that attracted more than 250,000 applications, of which 3,000 were accepted for trips. Why is this happening? The owner of the company believes that young people want "richer experiences" because the Internet connects people while reducing actual, real-life interpersonal relationships. "Voluntourism allows participants to engage with local communities and do things together.".[130] Contact is not real friendship. As we see with assisted living arrangements, the elderly fare much better when in a community instead of being alone. Volunteering provides a sense of self-worth while at the same time creating worthwhile benefits for others. We volunteer for many reasons. But, it is an activity that helps the individual feel good while helping others to feel better. This paradox is about being part of a solution.

The impact of this paradox affects corporations in a more vigorous way than ever. It used to be that corporations were called upon to be good citizens when it came to resources, the eco-consciousness era: being green, and actually behaving in an environmentally sound manner while managing the impact of an environmentally-sound global footprint. Consumers and observers recognize the difference between mere articulation of good green-speak (green-washing), and, actual behavior. Hotels would profess their eco-consciousness by asking the guest to decide whether or not the sheets and towels needed to be replaced every day.

Over the past decade or so, the corporate landscape has changed in many remarkable ways. Corporate Social Responsibility is a vocal and visible output of enterprises around the world. It is expected that organizations be "good-doers" and not just give back but improve. "Consumers around the world are saying loud and clear that a brand's social purpose is among the factors that influence purchase decisions. This behavior is on the rise and it provides opportunities for meaningful impact in our communities, in addition to helping to grow share for brands."[131]

The individual and interdependent paradox of The Age of I can affect organizational CSR. Should an organization consider cause-related marketing or corporate philanthropy? A study from 2016 discusses the differences of cause-related marketing (a company donating a part of the price paid for a product or service to a cause) relative to corporate philanthropy (a company making a lump sum to a charity). Those who emphasize their personal individuality more than their group interdependency tend to prefer companies to make charitable donations because they do not like having a company telling them what do. Those who emphasize their community identities over their personal self prefer cause-related marketing because they want to be part of a group.[132] Some responses are cultural. There are nations where the "group" identity culture is more forceful than the "independent" identity culture, and vice versa. The dimensions of The Age of I impact a multitude of institutions.

The fashion industry has not been known for planet-loving behaviors with the exception of pioneers such as Stella McCartney, Patagonia®, Katharine Hamnett, and Vivienne Westwood. The fashion industry is considered to be one of the worst polluting businesses, when considering leather, shearling, cotton, and other fabrics, and dyes, as well as low-cost labor. But now, according to *The Economist 1843*, the magazine of ideas, lifestyle, and culture, LVMH and Kering, the two largest fashion groups, are committing to a reduction in their environmental footprints. *The Economist 1843* posits that we should not blame the industry without looking at our own behaviors. And, it suggests that perhaps we follow the mantra of Vivienne Westwood who states, "buy better, and buy less."[133]

There is another way to understand this paradox of "doing good for me" and "doing good for the planet." Recent thinking from the public policy arena indicates that "mindful consumption is the way to heal ourselves and to heal the world." Mindfulness is fast becoming an antidote for a lot of what ails us. The team behind this public policy thinking believes that mindless consumption is physically and emotionally damaging for individuals as it generates bad behaviors, resource waste, and physical ailments. Do I really need to take another paper towel when a dishtowel would be better? Do I really want another case of water in 8 oz. bottles when a portable refillable bottle would be better? Do I really need to have the air conditioning at 68 degrees when 72 degrees would conserve valuable energy and be cleaner?

The paper indicates that mindless consumption defines the influence of impulsiveness, addiction, bad habits, compulsive behaviors and biased decision-making. Mindless eating is unhealthy, and leads to increased medical issues, which lead to the macro pharmacological ailments we face: it is your hand in the bowl of M&M's, or the bag of Doritos, without your paying attention to how much you are consuming. These policy researchers believe that awareness and paying attention to personal actions, being "in the moment" and non-judgmental will encourage people to behave better through self-regulation.[134] Not only will we be healthier individuals, we will not be wasteful when it comes to natural, personal, and financial resources. Further, if we are non-judgmental, we will avoid bias towards ethnic, religious, cultural differences generating better, healthier personal, national, and global relationships.

Mindfulness is a top-of-mind subject today. It has become a huge business from selling classes, vacations, spa treatments, books, tapes, DVDs, tea, and other foodstuffs as well a wide array of apps. But, rather than thinking of mindfulness as designed for personal betterment, mindfulness is now considered to be a part of maximizing the **Improve Me and Improve We** paradox. The consequences of mindless consumption are bigger than each of us.

The brand-business implications of the **Improve Me and Improve We** paradox are immense. These require maximizing benefits for the user and employee as well as benefits for the neighborhood, the community at large, the nation and planet. Whether you define it as the Consciousness Economy or Socially Conscious Consumption or Consumption with a Conscience or Principle-Based or Purposeful

Consumption, people are listening, watching, and evaluating the effects of brand-business behavior. How a brand or business behaves increasingly has an effect on the workplace as well as the world. Data on Millennials indicate that they prefer to work for enterprises based on the company's sense of purpose.[135] In the quest for enduring profitable growth, brand-business strategies and behaviors must maximize doing well *and* doing good. Paul Pollman CEO of Unilever said in an extensive article (*Forbes*, March 1, 2017) that the continuously activated sustainability policies and values of doing good things has been very influential when recruiting Millennials, "who want to work for a company that is engaged in the world."[136]

Kimbal Musk says he has created a restaurant concept called Next Door, an "urban casual" environment that will focus on America's heartland states. The restaurant, which has three locations so far but is expected to introduce fifty more, serves "real food" and, he describes real food as, "… Food you trust to nourish your body, nourish the farmer and nourish the planet."[137]

A recent *New York Times Style Review* carried advertisements from several companies that offer easy ways for customers to feel good by doing good. These are: 1) Chantecaille, a makeup brand sold at high-end retail stores such as Barney's New York, Bergdorf Goodman, Neiman Marcus, Nordstrom, Saks Fifth Avenue, and Net-a-Porter. The brand created three matte eye shadows dedicated to three women who lead conservation projects. The copy states, "Mattes That Matter. At Chantecaille we are passionate about conservation. This spring we're sharing the stories of three brilliant women who are game-changers in their field, each striving to protect our beloved animals." A share of your purchase money goes to these groups. There is an associated website where interested customers can learn more about this initiative. 2) An advertisement from emeco.net that sells a chair made from 111 recycled plastic bottles. The chair is featured with the word "rubbish" above it. 3) A United Kingdom-based gemstone company called Gemfields offers, "Responsibly sourced Mozambican rubies." 4) Swedish clothing designer Gundrun Sjödén offers a Spring collection described as, "All in nature's own sustainable materials for the world's colorful women." The advertisement features the "Jaquard knit in eco-cotton."[138]

INNOVATIVE AND DEPENDABLE

Samsung Note 7 smartphones, Samsung washing machines, Tesla autonomous car functions, constant downloading of patches for Microsoft products, and new cars that are recalled: our most innovative products may not always be the most dependable. And, yet, people want to know that the new product or service they are buying or interacting with will work as promised. It is not a cliché to say that we do wish for things to work, work well, and work well over time.

Many of us may be jaded about dependable innovations as we weather the frequent downloads that we need to install after a bug has been found in software. Some of us may be old enough to remember what it was like when starting your car was iffy. When Jaguar was a British car company before Ford and Tata, the beautiful cars spent a lot of time in your mechanic's care. Everyone who owned one knew the problems, and the car was a butt of many jokes. The owner base declined. Frequent global travelers wonder why Global Entry gives them a ticket with the dreaded XXX, indicating that they have to stand on a "special" line, when they have filled out a lengthy questionnaire, been finger-printed, photographed, and had an in-person interview thoroughly vetting and validating their trustworthiness. They have learned to expect the glitch that can happen on a regular basis.

Dependable innovation is an important enough topic now that Glasgow, Scotland's University of Strathclyde Business School offers a Master of Science degree on the subject called Project Management and Innovation. In 2015, Professor Luciana Dadderio posted a note on the Business School's website that stated the following:

> "My research on Dependable Innovation highlights how, in the current economic climate, firms are

increasingly faced with the difficult task of managing and resolving tensions that often appear paradoxical: they have to be innovative while at the same time being dependable... they must strive to lower costs and decrease time to market, but never at the expense of quality." [139]

Service innovations must be dependable as well. Dependability means that the service must be consistent, predictable, quality, competent, and satisfying. This makes the service credible. If the service differs each time, as with a product, its promise is no longer credible. Communicating one thing and delivering another affects the innovation's believability. Before Global Entry, in the 1990s, United States Customs and Border Patrol had a different, new, state-of-the-art system that provided a card based on interviews and full handprints to be used with the kiosk at immigration. Frequent travelers knew it rarely worked. But many tried anyway before giving up, and getting in a long line. In one case, a traveller renewing the service at JFK gave her handprint and card to the agent in the office only to see that the person on the screen with her name and data was a man. And, remember, it was the move to "innovative" yet not dependable financial securities that powered the recent financial meltdown.

A great deal of our innovation today is in the technological and digital arena. So, another way to think about this paradox is **Technology and Comfort**. Technology is always changing. It progresses at accelerating speeds. It is always new. And that newness and innovation should be comforting not scary. Comfort means there is assurance. New technologies may appear to be less than comforting. They may not be easy-to-use. They may make us feel dumb or uncomfortable.

One area where technology and comfort must be maximized is in the smart home. New innovative products that provide new innovative services must be reliable and offer comfort. There must be no tyranny of technology when delivering within the comforts of home. The products must not be too technical, and must not have so many features that a user manual is needed for proper operation. In other words, when it comes to the paradox of technology and comfort, the product or service technology must not be too technological.

Work conducted with a client in the appliance industry showed that something as simple as a washing machine could cause the user to feel unintelligent. The rinse-soak-wash choices required too much thinking. And, the options for the wash cycle did not match the user's natural language. In attempting to provide rinse-soak-wash options for all sorts of fabrics, and levels of dirt, the washing machines became disconnected from the user's reality. The question became, "Is it better to have multiple options or a simple one-button machine?"

Articles from the recent CES (Consumer Electronics Show) in January 2017 indicate that "easy-to-use" is part of the belief system within a lot of new technological and digital products and services. Some examples are:

- Connected car systems will be "easy-to-use."[140] A Ford SYNC®-equipped vehicle will be connected to a Samsung Gear S2 or new S3 smartwatch letting the driver receive parking space announcements and alerts to keep drivers attentive while driving. "The easy-to-use" feature means that you don't have to remember to take out your smartphone, and note your parking location. Rather, the app proactively asks you to log the vehicle's location with just a few taps on your watch."[141]
- Panasonic introduced a new Countertop Induction Oven using their innovations in heating technology "that allows the oven to grill, bake, re-heat with little or no pre-heating, resulting in perfectly cooked meals." The Panasonic PR release stated that this new Countertop Induction Oven "… is an example of food-tech at its best. It delivers a quick, yet high-end and healthy cooking experience to consumers in a compact, easy-to-use design."[142]

- The world's first automatic grill-cleaning robot that is Bluetooth enabled was introduced. The Grillbot Pro is "... easy-to-use and will deliver the hands-free cleaning experience that the original Grillbot provides as well as the following new features: Bluetooth 4.0 technology and smartphone app that allows control of certain functions from a smartphone while away from the grill."[143]

However, "easy to use" is not enough. Ease is a multi-dimensional concept. Innovators, brands, individuals, organizations, and others have to recognize that it is essential to deliver on the Three Dimensions of Ease: ease of choice, ease of use, and ease of mind. The proliferation of product and service options, and the diffusion of accelerating technologies have made decision-making more difficult than ever. Information overload sometimes confuses rather than confirms, making decision-making uncertain. We find ourselves in decision-making overload.

THE THREE DIMENSIONS OF EASE

EASE OF CHOICE

Choice should be easy. We want more choice, and more personalization. But, we want choosing to be simple. Making a choice should be easy. It should require a minimum effort, and not take a lot of time. We do not want to spend a lot of time on a choice that should not take huge amount of energy to make. In other words, we do not want increased mental and physical effort.

We do not want decreases in the speed of our decision-making. We live in a world of "now," and that means we have expectations about making good, satisfying decisions quickly. *Euromonitor International*, a supplier of global market research covering thousands of products and services, indicated in 2014 that there has been an increasing contraction in the space between first product/service interest and actual purchase.[144] Our current technologies allow us to swipe an icon to make an immediate purchase on our smartphone. We have become used to "instant" choice satisfaction. The idea of slowing down to make a choice is agonizing. Apps and Amazon have made selection immediate. We are rewarded with immediate gratification.

In many American grocery stores, the concept of nutritious snacks is claiming the aisles. To understand the quandary of choice, stand in front of the chips-pretzels aisle. Unless you already know your favorite brand and variety, you will probably become overcome and dazed. Among the highly salted, high potassium-laden potato snacks; and corn tortilla chips in blue, red, yellow or white; the cheese puffs, twists, baked or fried; and the pretzel sticks, nuggets, twists (tiny or large, cheese or peanut butter filled) are the chickpea, soy, lentil, and black bean chips.

Or attempt to buy a toothbrush: first, do you want an electric toothbrush or a manual one? Do you have a brand that you prefer? Which size brush head do you prefer? Do you want a soft, medium or hard brush head? Do you prefer a round brush or a rectangular brush? What color do you want? Do you want a battery-charging stand?

Forget trying to make a quick confident choice in the pet food aisle: when there are entire stores dedicated to pet care, the choices are endless. For cats and dogs, it used to be just wet or dry, bagged or canned. But, now you can purchase food in pouches, fresh food in the chill-case, food by age of pet, breed of pet, size of pet, health of pet, weight of pet, bad breath of pet, mental health of pet, and combinations of these ingredients. There are snacks for pets, dry, soft or filled.

Ease of Use

We should live in a user-manual-free world. Service options should not require a lot of explanation. Once we *easily* choose, use of the product or service should be easy. People have enough going on in their lives: they do not need to waste precious time and energy on learning how to use or navigate a product or service. It is the role of the provider to take the complexity out of choice as well as the use. Further, overly complicated products and services cause us to feel inept or inadequate, and, sometimes, cause us to feel stupid.

One reason Millennials are shunning home purchase is that they see ownership as onerous with too many commitments and constraints that sap time, energy, and money. In the sharing economy, we do not have to own: we can rent. We can avoid owning a car; we can avoid owning a vacation home, or a boat, or a plane. We can avoid owning fancy dresses, or accessories. We can avoid insurance, taxes, and commitments. We want our choices to be easy to use so we opt for access over ownership.

Apple made computers easy to use, and then made mobile phones with cameras easy to use. They made music easily available on those phones. Amazon made buying books, and then, practically anything else easy and fast, and Amazon continues to expand and improve. A recent shopping list on Amazon included such disparate items as a bag of dried Carolina Reaper peppers, the new book, *Lincoln in the Bardo*, a pair of therapeutic gloves, a bottle of non-soy B vitamins, and a large box of Wine Gums. Netflix makes going to the movies easy. FedEx made it easy and dependable to send mail and packages overnight. Blue Apron makes cooking from scratch easy.

In a San Francisco, California, pilot program, Volvo now offers owners of its XC90 SUV and S90 luxury sedan models a concierge service where, for example, you park your car at your office, and when you leave at the end of the day, your car has been serviced, cleaned, and refueled. The program allows participating owners contact with concierge services in their vicinity so they can order services they like via their Volvo smartphone app. Volvo Car Group's VP of Consumer Connectivity Services, Anders Tylman-Mikiewicz says,

> "Our approach is a simple one – we aim to make life easier by employing the latest connected technology in an easy-to-use smartphone app. We are taking an open and agile approach to this and welcome collaboration with new partners and innovative service offers. This is just the beginning."[145]

A tax preparation company facing declining customer traffic conducted a study to understand the problems consumers have with tax preparation. There were hundreds of problems, and aside from the problem of having to send money to the IRS, the most important, frequently occurring problems had to do with ease of understanding tax preparation language: the language was mystifying. Potential customers wanted the language to be understandable: this would make it easier to use the tax prep provider's services. And, would help them feel more comfortable about the entire stressful process.

The Dutch GPS Company, TomTom has ease of use in its mission statement. It states,

> "Our mission is to make technology so easy to use that everyone can benefit from it." Additionally, it says, "We created easy to use navigation devices, helping millions of people to get where they want to be. Today, we simplify the complex, making technology more accessible for everyone."[146]

Ease of use is essential, especially when it involves technology. Many companies get this right. But, then there are those companies that seem to make it more difficult, on purpose. Kate Murphy at *The New York Times* wrote about the behavior and attitudes at cable and mobile service companies in July 2016. The article stated that these companies monetize every second of every interaction. As people become more tech-savvy, they call when the problems are more complex, requiring more time. Call service employees are on a cost-per-contact model, which is why a call may be shifted from one agent to another. And, if you ask for a supervisor, in many cases you wind up speaking to just another agent who has been alerted in advance.[147]

The goal is to get you off the phone quickly rather than get your problem fixed.

Technology and Comfort, Innovation and Dependable are must-do paradoxes that need to be maximized in design and delivery of products and services. However, there is a third dimension of ease that must be worked into the equation to truly optimize these paradoxes: ease of mind.

Ease of Mind

It is not enough to be easy to choose and easy to use. People want to feel comfortable with their decision. They want to feel reassured that they made the right choice. "Am I comfortable with the decision? Now that I am using this product or service, am I satisfied with the choice?" Am I doing the right thing for me? Am I doing the right thing for my family? Am I doing the right thing for my pet? Am I doing the right thing for the community? Am I doing the right thing for future generations? People want to feel right about their decisions rather than feel regret. And, people want to know that the brands and organizations with which they do business are doing the right thing. Are employees treated properly? Is the company a good global citizen? Does the company have my best interests in mind? Is the brand or the company a decent contributor to my communities? Are the brand and corporate leaders making ethical decisions?

There is a concept called Prospect Theory that describes how people tend to prefer making decisions that are defined as "gains" rather than "losses." In business, this means framing the decisions in terms of profitability. This focus on "is the decision going to make money" can result in decisions that are biased against things like environmental concern.[148]

Global Monitor, The Futures Company's annual survey, indicated that over the years, people believe that, "If the opportunity arises, most businesses will take advantage of the public, if they feel they are not likely to be found out."[149] This affects purchasing. If people feel uncomfortable, they may avoid buying products and services from companies whose motives they question.

At this writing, Chipotle is working to regain customer trust that was lost when the brand experienced the multiple outbreaks of E-coli in its restaurants. Customers have to feel at ease about choosing to eat there. How would you feel about driving a car with a Takata airbag? Exxon and BP experienced horrific oil spills: did you stop refueling your car at their gas stations because of these incidents? Are you comfortable flying on United Airlines?

As we mentioned, people do not want to feel stupid. If the product is so complex or confusing to use, we do not feel comfortable. Once again, we humans are pain avoidance mammals. Discomfort is painful; feeling ill at ease is distressing. We will avoid interacting with products and services that make us feel uncomfortable.

There is another reason to address the three dimensions of ease. It is based on work conducted by Nobel Prize winner Herbert Simon in 1956. Professor Simon's focus was the decision-making process. He coined a word, "satisficing" that is a blend of satisfy and suffice. Satisficing is a decision-making strategy that attempts to meet criteria for adequacy rather than to identify an optimal solution. In situations where there are many choices or many choices are presented one by one, finding the best choice can be a hopeless quest. We become stymied: we will opt for the first choice or opt for a choice that appears to address the most needs. In either case, we do not make the best choice. Additionally, our inherent desire to make simple, effortless choices in the face of too many, uncertain options, forces us to default to the cheapest, the most expensive, or whatever choice feels satisfactory whether it is best or not.

In a world where information is available in real, immediate time, spending time on an innovation's dependability technology is critical. And, yet, as events show, competitiveness, time to market, being first, and analyst-shareholder pressures can force beta testing to be compressed or overlooked, or, as in the case of Volkswagen's emission scandal, faked. Was it that important to be #1 at the expense of harming people, and harming the planet by falsifying information about the vehicles' emissions systems?

SAFE AND ADVENTURE

Not everyone is a candidate for extreme sports. Not everyone is physically fit enough for Ninja Warrior. Not everyone can afford to travel to Europe. But, that does not mean that we want to eliminate excitement and adventure from our lives. In an uncertain and precarious world, having the opportunity to be adventurous with a little bit of risk is desirable.

The maximization of safe *and* adventure is well addressed in the travel industry. Type in "safe adventure travel" while on Google, and dozens of options pop-up: for example, Endless Turns has a safe adventure mission statement on its Internet homepage:

> "Endless Turns Ski & Adventure Travel offers ski and adventure travel trips throughout North & South America. We provide our travelers with in-depth knowledge and expertise when arranging each adventure. We believe the most memorable travels

include authentic cultural experiences and a safe adventure."[150]

And, Developing World Connections, a vacation volunteer site, also cites "safe adventure" as part of their mantra for people who want to have a good time and help others.[151] Disney pioneered safe adventure. Its theme parks, cruises and resorts offer the magic and celebration of a child's adventure with just that little bit of thrill. Other amusement parks have "thrill" rides. SeaWorld had its live orca shows, the Shamu Experience, where the tiny risk for the viewers was to don a plastic rain parka (you were so close to the orcas that you would be splashed and sodden during the show). If you wished to spend more money, you could have "lunch" with Shamu, and sit in a protected restaurant area next to the pool eating buffet lunch while the trainers brought the whales around for you to see up close. As an amazing piece of branding an experience, a teenage girl who had spent her tween life trying to save Willy, attended the lunch with her mother fully expecting to see Shamu. She was horrified to learn that Shamu had been dead for years and was not in the pool. Shamu was long gone but The Shamu Experience lived on.

Have you ever wanted to be a mermaid? At Weeki Wachee Springs State Park in western Florida, home of the live mermaids, children and adults can fulfill a "safe" dream adventure by enrolling in Junior Mermaid Camp, for the kids, or in Sirens of the Deep Mermaid camp for the 30-years old and older group.

The burgeoning virtual reality gaming and experience business is based on a kind of safe adventure. With virtual (VR) reality, you can be adventurous, actually be *in the* adventure without being harmed because you are probably at your desk or on your couch. Travel is betting on VR to generate a destination "experience" hoping that once you go into the destination virtually, you will opt to actually travel there. As described by Janet Levere, tourist companies and countries find that VR can provide the tantalizing experience in a safe environment so potential visitors can "test drive" the adventure before embarkation.[152]

Beyond an actual VR game, there are now places where you can go to join in a VR game. One example is Kalahari Resorts and Conventions. In several of its locations it has The Arena, an interactive, virtual reality experience that is more than just a video game.

> The Arena is a "free-roam, warehouse-scale, multiplayer, virtual reality gaming experience currently on the market. Multiplayer adventures allow up to six people to simultaneously explore, conquer and challenge one another for high scores and skill evaluations, all tracking in real time."[153]

For the Cartoon Network set, safe adventure via VR has penetrated the animated series *Adventure Time*. Geek.com (of all sources!) reviewed Adventure Time praising an episode that featured VR. The writer reports on the episode, "Imaginary Resources," where the protagonist boy and his dog put on VR headsets, as follows:

> "… It's also a well-handled commentary on technology dependence. The players are humans who have chosen the Better Reality over the real one outside. Friendly mechanical butterflies tend to their basic needs and give their muscles a workout from time to time. They spend all their time in the game. It's easy to escape into our technology when real life gets too hard to deal with. This from a cartoon featuring a talking dog and sentient desserts."[154]

Do you want to change the world? Can you do this adventurous task without risk? Well, yes, now you can. Maximizing the needs for adventure and safety, Singapore's ArtScience Museum at Marina Bay Sands, a premiere cultural institution in Southeast Asia, now has an interactive exhibit called *Into the Wild*. This exhibit is a virtual rainforest that visitors explore with a smartphone device.

> "The virtual adventure becomes a reality, when visitors take an active role in replanting the rainforests of Southeast Asia. For every virtual tree planted, and accompanied with a pledge to WWF (World Wildlife Fund), a real tree will be planted in a rainforest in Indonesia."[155]

For decades, the fragrance industry has supplied safe adventure to women and men. The names and images as well as the bottle designs have offered people an acceptable way to feel risky and, yes, risqué. Yves Saint Laurent has Black Opium, Dior has Sauvage, Chantecalle has Le Wild, and there is an offering called Wild Attitude. In 2015, shoemaker Jimmy Choo launched a fragrance brand called Illicit. It was described as a fragrance,

> "... For the woman who does not live her life by trends and does what she wants... an edgy, liberated, yet seductive persona... a tempting, seductive Illicit woman with bold style, rebellious attitude and unabashed nature."[156]

The fashion industry has also afforded us the chance to feel adventurous. From shoes to lingerie to street-style wear, or biker-chic, we can take a small chance by donning something just a bit naughty. One of the reasons we see frequent 1960s and 1970s clothing styles is the freedom and adventurousness of the designs. We can feel daring for a moment of satin, yellow bell-bottoms, or tie-dyed anything, or Pucci swirls.

SUVs stir up a sense of adventure. The Nissan Xterra was designed for mud-coated, off-road, physically demanding outdoor activities. The Toyota RAV4 was originally a small SUV driven by young women.

Now, *Automotive News* states that Toyota is offering a new version called RAV4 Adventure. The new version will have a roof rack, lower bodyguards and a small lift in height. There will also be a towing package, and changes to the radiator and cooling system. Toyota says that they want to imbue the vehicle with a little of their truck DNA but it will still be a "soft roader" rather than a "rock climber." The RAV4 Adventure is for a slightly more rugged yet safe sensibility.[157]

Only 36 percent of Americans have passports.[158] There are many reasons for not traveling abroad. Some feel their current environment is very diverse. Some prefer domestic travel. Fear is another reason people do not leave the United States.[159] Traveling can be a risk, especially in an unpredictable, changeable world. For those who have no interest in traveling to Venice, New York or Paris, you can experience these cities in Las Vegas. The gondolas in the "canal" of the Venetian can transport you to Italy.

In an uncertain world, we are less likely to take chances and more likely to find ways in which we can feel safe with a little spice. As technology advances, we will have more opportunities to be virtually daring, while staying secure in reality.

Summary

There are numerous paradoxes that can be addressed by brand and business. Our list is long but certainly not the be-all-and-end-all. In politics, social issues, and other aspects of daily life, there are paradoxes: but these are out of scope for this book.

Paradoxes for Paradox Promise Solutions

- Connection and Disconnection
    - Alone and Together
- Delay and Desire
- Timeliness and Timelessness

- Abundant and Rare
  - Exclusive and Affordable
- Personalization (automated) and Personal (human)
- Privacy and Personalization
  - Preserving Anonymity and Wanting to Be Known
- Technological Control and Human Control
  - Do It For Me In My Way and Do It For Myself
- Indulgence and Wellness
  - Diet and Delight
- Improved Me and Improved We
- Innovation and Dependable
  - Technology and Comfort
- The Three Dimensions of Ease
  - Ease of Choice
  - Ease of Use
  - Ease of Mind
- Safe and Adventure

PART 3

PRINCIPLES FOR FINDING PARADOXES AND GENERATING PARADOX PROMISES

Finding the paradoxes that make sense for your brand or business takes discipline and creativity. It requires a diverse group of thinkers and observers who reflect thought processes different from analytics. Seeking the paradoxes is not about forecasting; it is about having foresight.

We identify nine principles that will help your search for paradoxes. These nine principles will also help in developing Paradox Promises. Finding the paradoxes means uncovering the customer's contradictory needs. A Paradox Promise maximizes these needs into a relevant, differentiating, trustworthy (brand) experience. These rules may seem simple but they require changes to the way we look at information, how we generate knowledge and ideas from the information, how we build the desired customer experiences, and how we organize the enterprise to accept and implement the Paradox Promises.

We also provide some brand and business stories to explain the principle.

1. Look for the Little Things

Sometimes it is not the big things that matter most. Learning to look for the little things changes the way you see.

In 2002, John Nagl wrote a book on counterinsurgency. He makes the point that during the Vietnam era, fighting small wars was not recognized as an essential aspect of the army's business. The US Army continued to view its performance against larger wars.[160] Small wars require different tactics and require alternate ways of perceiving things.

The point is that big scale and scope have merits but so do small scale and scope. And, when identifying paradoxes, there may be small things going on in various places that could be a foretaste of a bigger idea. It also entails knowing how to see (*saper vedere*), which was Leonardo Da Vinci's credo (thinking strategy) about creating.

Newspaper: Being New and Time-Honored Every Day

In 1995, our work with one of the nation's most venerable newspapers uncovered a very small idea within a sea of collected data, an idea that changed the trajectory of the paper's communications to its readers. In those days, the marketing approach was to focus on new subscribers. Potential readers were offered great subscription deals. However, its passionate readers, those people who cannot start their day without reading it, were being ignored, taken for granted.

Passionate loyalists had many reasons for loving and needing the newspaper. One interesting reason for this passion was mentioned just a few times, hidden within all sorts of other rationales. People read the paper and felt well informed, current, and complete. Loyal readers always found something in the paper that they could discuss with others at a cocktail party, a café, or over dinner, or drinks. And, this discovered story or report made these loyalists feel smarter, satisfied, and more confident. These loyalists were curious and valued education and learning. They appreciated the intellectual stimulation the paper provided. Here was a single product that provided multiple benefits not just for the day, but also for life. They perceived the paper as helping to improve them. Each day loyalists received something new while knowing the source was time-honored and enduring.

C AMEL: B ELONG TO THE W ORLD AND B E S OLITARY

The Surgeon General's Report linking smoking to health issues was released in 1964. In the early 1970s, the tobacco companies were still dealing with the ways in which they would be communicating their brands. Cigarette television advertising was no more. The tobacco companies poured their money into print and outdoor options. Packages, print ads, and billboards now had a warning box. All cigarette communications had to work within the new Surgeon General's guidelines.

Camel's major competitor was Philip Morris' Marlboro. (Philip Morris also owned Miller Beer.) Marlboro was a massively popular brand with a most incredible, indelible image.

There was something interesting in the Marlboro print ads, and the Miller Beer TV ads. One intriguing observation was that both Miller Beer and Marlboro were using a similar approach: give the smoker (drinker) a place in time where men (the target audience) smoke and/or drink for pleasure. Philip Morris made a time in a man's day into a place for him to be: reinforcing that there are special times in a man's day when it is time to relax and smoke (or drink). For Marlboro, it was Marlboro Country. The cowboy out on the range, at the bunkhouse, or by the campfire with a Marlboro and his leather gloves, reins, and/or horse. For Miller Beer, Miller created Miller Time with its masculine camaraderie. Beer could advertise on television, so by 1980, the Miller Time advertising became reminiscent of Marlboro with a western setting and a tag line, "Down toward home and a place called Miller Time."

These observations may seem small. But, hidden in the competitors' communications was an opportunity for the Camel man.

The Marlboro man was a cowboy; he was rugged, independent, and always working. He had a place to relax and enjoy himself aside from his job. He lived in a place that never changed, the American West. The Marlboro man evoked our westward, hard-working individualism, and traditional values. When smoking a Marlboro, people could feel connected to this image of strong individualism: it could provide a self-image of pure, independent, rugged strength.

The Camel man was different. The Camel man belonged to the world while being a modern, solitary adventurer with an instinctive, visceral sense of life. He lived in the bigger, more exotic world. He already had the psychological space for relaxation and smoking enjoyment because his rugged, outdoor environment was that place in time, "Where a man belongs." All Camel communications showed the Camel man in outdoor, rough yet beautiful, far away, sometimes mysterious, glamorous, colorful landscapes. Yet, when smoking a Camel, one could feel that as strong-minded individuals they were cosmopolitan, belonging to an international, multi-cultural world.

2. Look for ideas outside of your standard social media circles, favorite periodicals, e-zines, information sites and journals

Take information and learn from all areas: arts, science, technology, financial, political, academic, and medical. Look across geography. Ideas are borderless. Listen outside of your comfortable echo chamber. As Luc de Clapiers, Marquis de Vauvenargues (a writer and moralist in the early 1700's, known for his aphorisms) said, "Most people grow old within a small circle of ideas, which they have not discovered for themselves." Singular expertise and its knowledge can create a kind of conceptual inertia that stops us thinking creatively.

Analytics is acceptable but synthesis, and non-linear thinking will be required. Harvard University's Howard Gardner looked at non-linear thinkers in his work on *Five Minds for the Future*. He identified the Disciplinary Mind ("mastery of major schools of thought, including science, mathematics, and history, and of at least one professional craft"); the Synthesizing Mind ("ability to integrate ideas from different disciplines or spheres into a coherent whole and to communicate that integration to others"); the Creating Mind ("capacity to uncover and clarify new problems, questions, and phenomena"); the Respectful Mind ("awareness of and appreciation for differences among human beings and human groups"); and the Ethical Mind ("fulfillment of one's responsibilities as a worker and as a citizen").[161]

He gave a speech on the subject in 2008, where he said that non-linear thinking is in its ascendancy, and this is important because it is something that cannot (yet) be automated. In his review of the five minds, one of the aspects that make these types of thinkers intriguing is the ability to look across disciplines. For the synthesizing mind, Dr. Gardner highlights Charles Darwin who he describes as a masterful synthesizer. He recounts that Charles Darwin was at sea on the *Beagle* for five years gathering a vast trove of information on flora and fauna. He conducted experiments and learned from as many naturalists as possible. And then, after 20 years, Darwin wrote his "great intellectual syntheses *On the Origin of the Species*."[162]

Looking across disciplines and information for ideas, and elements of interest, is good. But today, we are inundated with information. So, it is important to find those thinkers who can sift through and pluck out what is going to be useful.

CHOCOLATE FILL BAR: FILL THE HUNGER-HOLE IN YOUR STOMACH WITHOUT BEING FILLING

We worked with a global confectionary company in the 1990's. At the time, the company was up-dating the brand promises of its major brands. A senior executive came to the United States to participate in the process. One afternoon, he took a stroll through a shopping mall near the company's headquarters. He noticed that young adults were walking around the mall with portable snacks, none of which were candy bars. He noticed that there were slices of pizza, large cookies,

French fries, bags of salty chips, and popcorn. He recounted this story as we were thinking about the brand's benefits. The young adults in the mall were hungry. They found foods to satiate their hunger. Our chocolate fill bar product could easily have been an option. It was delicious, filling, and hunger satisfying. But, we viewed the competitive set as other confectionary products. The executive's observation from outside of our comfort zone made us rethink the brand's competitive set. In doing so, the brand became anytime food, satisfying intrusive hunger as a perfect fill. After all, it was more portable than a pizza slice (you could put it in a backpack or briefcase), and its ingredients were more satiating than a bag of chips or French fries. The bar filled up the hunger hole in your stomach without being filling so you could get on with your important activities.

McDonald's: Forever and Young

After a month of intensive review, and synthesis of all of the McDonald's global segmentation research (as far back as the 1970s), we were ready to generate a new brand promise that would stay within the brand's framework but be more relevant to consumers. We identified the paradox of the McDonald's brand. We understood that the brand dynamics were: Inclusivity and Individuality; Global and Local; Predictable and Spontaneous; Consistent and Changing (been there for you yet reflects where you are now in your life); Familiar and New; and, Stable and Dynamic. But we were struggling to find an idea that would capture these dichotomies. We looked to Bob Dylan. Rather than stay within the comfort zone of our information, and knowledge set, we went to a place where a master of ideas put into words resides. It was our feeling that the paradoxes of the McDonald's brand all had one thing in common: Forever and Young. McDonald's had tradition, familiarity and had been a part of people's lives from childhood to the present. At the same time, McDonald's was fresh, contemporary, a place of new foods and beverages that satisfy an individual's eating needs. The brand experience came from its special character, being forever young, offering what no one else could offer: the delight of a familiar predictable yet contemporary way to eat.

3. Differentiate information from trends from insights

Language is important. If we are to work together across functions and geographies, it is necessary that we have the same definitions of words. Organizations need a common language so that words, such as quality or loyalty, mean the same thing throughout the enterprise. We worked with one industrial client where every country had its own definition of quality.

In the same way that organizations use the same words for their financial affairs, organizations must have a common language for their brands as well. When it comes to information, trends and insights, we have created a muddled linguistic situation. Not only do we tend to use these terms interchangeably but also, we overuse and misuse the word "insight."

Why does this matter? It matters because there is a relationship between information and trends, and trends and insights. Information happens first. It leads to the generation of trends, which then lead to the creation of insights. It is a process that sets the context for creativity. It does not create paradoxes but provides the framework for helping to figure out paradoxes.

Information is the facts. And, in our data processing world, information is data that are processed, stored and/or communicated. We have massive amounts of data being processed into massive amounts of information. Demographics are information, for example. From the standpoint of seeking paradoxes, we need to take the information, and, using various ways of thinking, formulate trends.

A trend is something that is developing or changing. A trend is enduring. A trend is an idea or concept that is happening around us, and influencing the way and manner in which we behave. For example, a trend in demographics is that women in many developed countries are having children later in life or are having only one child.

Another demographic trend is that many Millennials live with their parents. Trends have implications, of course. And we can generate strategies to address these trends.

But, trends are not insights. Trends are valuable because they inform us about the world around us. But, collecting and analyzing information, and turning these into trends are not enough. We must go from information to insight. Informed insight is not guesswork. Insight means seeing below the surface of information. Insight is all about "why?" This necessitates synthesizing rather than only analyzing. Analysis travels backward. But we are moving forward. So we must use synthesis. Synthesis means, "the combining of diverse concepts into a new coherent whole." Analysis leads to understanding what is happening and why. Synthesis leads to insight into what might happen.

Trends are general. It is the insight we have about the trends that is critical. It means looking under the surface, beyond appearances and seeing ahead. Meaningful insights are more than mere information, and trends.

Unfortunately, insight has become a marketing cliché; and, it is misunderstood, and misused. It has become a meaningless, useless term.

- Is it insight to discover that people's incomes are under strain and stress?
- Is it insight to learn that people want an easy-to-set-up mobile phone?
- Is it insight to learn that people like food that tastes good?
- Is it insight to learn that people prefer a dog food the dog will eat?
- Is it insight to learn that a business-to-business customer wants a computer system that will not crash?

These are not insights. These are observations of the obvious. Yet, in each case, these were reported as insights based on extensive research. A consumer insight is not what you always believed; it is not driven by what the factory makes; it is not just information or facts; nor is it product attributes.

An insight needs to meet two criteria: 1) Surprise at what you learned; and, 2) As a result, a change in behavior based on this learning. An insight is a fundamental consumer truth that has the power to open our eyes. It is relevant, recognizable, believable, ownable, adaptable to geographies, and capable of building business for the long-term.

Keeping with the demographics example, it is an insight to recognize that the world is getting older and younger at the same time. Due to this insight, brands/businesses will have to decide what their strategies will be to address these two cohorts. It is an insight to understand that with a large older and elderly population, the nature and management of military service, and attitudes toward war will change, and affect policy. Older people are more risk-averse.

CROWNE PLAZA WORKLIFE ROOM: BE COMFORTABLE WHILE BEING HIGHLY PRODUCTIVE

When we began working with IHG, one of the first projects we were given was the revitalization of the Crowne Plaza brand. We wrote about this briefly in our previous 2016 book.[163] Crowne Plaza made the decision to be a business hotel catering to ambitious business travelers for whom business success is the goal. At IHG, there was also a lot of research on how many of their guests were travelling on business or for pleasure. Business travelers have very specific needs.

Some trends that were happening at the time (2013-2014) were the increasing use of mobile, the increasing desire for connectivity, and the beginning impact of the sharing economy. Extensive research showed that these highly motivated travelers wanted to find some time to unwind, and feel comfortable, but they also wanted to be productive in their room. They had work to do, presentations to create, speeches to rehearse. However, the room should be comfortable, easy to use, and, if possible, there should be some separation of the workspace from the relax space and the sleep space. These travelers wanted a workspace that did not look like a cubicle. The key insight was a paradox: I want to feel so comfortable that I can actually be more productive when working. True comfort can help me work better for business and personal success. The brief to the design company was to create a hotel room that maximized the need to work productively *and* the need to feel incredibly comfortable. (NB: The London-based design consultancy, PearsonLloyd, immediately after the new hotel room project completion, put the entire Crown Plaza new room project up on their website as a sales piece-case study, www.pearsonlloyd.com)

European Appliance Company: Silent and Powerful

Finding a paradox is important, but it may not always work. Insight into the insight may be necessary. Understanding consumer problems, and then finding the best solutions may require additional root cause investigation and fishbone solutions work. This story is an example of an insight that "got away."

In the late 1970s General Electric ran commercials for a dishwasher that was so quiet a baby could sleep through the entire wash and rinse cycles. The dishwasher was a huge success and the advertisement was very well received. Noisy appliances have always been an issue. This is one of the reasons that some communities have special hours for leaf blowers. Airports have strict noise abatement rules, which is one reason why the Concorde could only takeoff and land in certain cities at certain times.

So, it was no surprise that our appliance client decided to make a vacuum cleaner that was quiet, almost silent, during use. There were a lot of research, data, information, and documentation from the engineers about how to create the silent vacuum. Additionally, there was the issue of whether it should use a bag, or be bagless like the new entry in the vacuum category, Dyson. How much suction should it have? How would silence affect suction? How long should the cord be? What shape was required? How many wheels should it have? At the time, the trends in Europe were for smaller vacuums, and battery-operated vacuums. The trend of women in the workforce meant that housekeeping might happen at odd hours, possibly when children were asleep. Silence would be appealing to families with children. A silent vacuum would be kinder to pets' ears. A silent vacuum cleaner would be less disruptive of the harmony of the living space. Our client identified situations for the quietest vacuum: hospitals, nursing homes, nurseries, hotels, as well as homes. The vacuum went into production.

At the same time, the Dyson brand was powering across the United Kingdom and into Europe with its expensive, high performing aggressive-looking, powerful sounding bagless product. The bagless Dyson vacuum solved two important, frequently occurring vacuum problems: 1) people could never find the proper bag for their vacuum in the store; and, 2) changing the vacuum cleaner bags was a disgusting, dusty mess. The Dyson design made the vacuum look like it would really work. And, it sounded like it was really working. It was not so much the decibel level; it was its type of powerful sound. In every European country it entered, it began to grow.

Our client believed that the quietest vacuum would be a big seller. It offered powerful suction but was quiet: powerful and quiet was the insight. Yet, this quietest vacuum was not selling well. Investigation pointed to something previously misinterpreted: with a vacuum, sound is necessary. Powerful sound indicates that the product is performing very well, sucking up all that dust and dirt. Silence or near silence made users think the product was not doing its job. The Dyson product roared with assertiveness. All the information along with the biases of the engineers led to an insight that was not quite complete. As we said before, sorting through the information is as important as the information itself. Or, as we like to say, the researcher is as important as the research.

4. There is no Formula for Creative Thinking

Regardless of what you hear and read, you need to start with creative thinkers. This, in itself, is a challenge because you cannot go up to someone and ask if they are creative, and expect to receive a good answer. As with a lot of things, creativity happens over time. Dr. Gardner says this about creative people:

> "People who are creative are those who come up with new things, which eventually get accepted. The only way that creativity can be judged is, if over the long run, the creator's works change how other people think and behave. That is the only criterion for creativity."[164]
>
> As the British advertising executive, Trevor Beattie, said, "Creativity is the wheel on your suitcase."

Creativity is not a product although it can wind up inspiring a product. It is a continuing, never-ending flow of imaginative ideas. Creativity brings into being something that was not there before. It offers a new perception by integrating, rearranging, and reordering familiar elements in unfamiliar ways. Creativity involves risk-taking and courage. At certain points in the creative act, we express what we are thinking and doing through a medium: film, video, music, artwork, and so forth. And, creativity changes us: whether we are viewing a painting in a museum, using an IPhone, or an Echo.

Creativity involves tension. The creative process lives off what Jerry Hirschberg, the founding director of Nissan Design International, calls creative abrasion.[165] It is comfort and uncomfortable at the same time. It is having pairs of divergent thinkers arguing and agreeing all at the same time. It is allowing dissenting viewpoints to be discussed while harnessing that friction. Creativity needs time, energy, and routine while at the same time it needs unbridled desire and liberty. In other words, creativity needs discipline and freedom. Discipline and freedom tug at each other: the more tugging the better.

Discipline and freedom are at the heart of our concept of Freedom within a Framework: the boundaries within which creative ideas flourish. But creative freedom lacks a formula. Each creative mind comes to their creativity in their own way. The problem is this: you can teach someone to play the piano through lessons and practice but you cannot teach everyone to be Mozart or Bach. You can take an art class or buy a camera but the odds of being Matisse or Ansel Adams are slim. The best we can hope for is an organization or community that is open to creativity, a culture that is conducive to creativity.

In most organizations there is some form of new product development process with principles, flow charts, arrows, research, and gates. Here is where formula and process are needed. This is also the place where obstacles surface and challenges arise. Product and service development processes are necessary structures. But, some can be so structured with so many steps, phases, decision points, gatekeepers, and activities that inputs may be unrecognizable if they ever even emerge into an investment request.

Toy Company: Safe Play and Brilliant Creativity

It is one thing to develop a creative organization. It is one thing to build time into employees' schedules for creativity such as at 3M. It is quite another thing when your vision, mission, brand platform and culture are a paean to nurturing creativity in growing children. The guiding principle of this toy company was that its products could help children develop creativity for their own good, and use that creativity later on in life for the good of the world. It was their vision that children who let their imaginations run wild could some day use that imagination to change the world. They believed that the creativity their products engendered could inspire the human spirit. These were non-technology toys mostly for toddlers. And yet, the company believed that they provided families with creative experiences, playing a small but significant role in sparking safe creative play leading to creative thinking. Their internal values of fun, learning, and simplicity reflected this passion for nurturing a child's ingenuity, inventiveness and resourcefulness. They did not see themselves as a manufacturer or a toy company but as an activist advocate for creativity.

A Process for Creativity? Formulated Creativity

This is a story about how we became the people who said *yes or no* to requests for investments in product renovations and innovations at a European durable goods company. But it is also a story about the paradox of formulated creativity.

It began with a needs-based global segmentation study. Within the segments, industrial design teams worked with managers to understand the users, users' needs, users' occasions, and users' problems to generate insights. These new understandings would drive new product-service ideas as well as renovations of existing products-services. A new product-service or a renovation would need an investment request that included a schedule, engineering reports, fit and finish details, and the amount of money desired.

The CEO decided that in order to make the organization more customer-centric, each investment request should have a consumer insight page. As long-time brand consultants with the company, we were asked to make a simple insight "questionnaire" that every person requesting *any* investment of *any amount* for a product project would have to answer.

Based on the discussion we had earlier on what is an insight, you can imagine how strange this task seemed: a template for insight? However, we believed that adding the consumer to the development or redevelopment of the product or service was fundamental. We agreed and created these four questions, which became the first page of the investment request package.

1. *What is the consumer insight?* Describe what you have learned about your consumer that has led you to develop this new product-service or renovate your existing product-service

2. *To what target consumer market segment(s) is this consumer insight relevant?* Identify the needs-based segment or segments to which this product-service is positioned
3. *What are the target consumer need(s)/problem(s) that we are addressing with this product-service?* Identify the need this product-service will satisfy or the problem this product-service will solve for the target consumer
4. *What are the product-service development requirements/ product-service renovations to operationalize this insight?* Identify the features you have designed and intend to manufacture that meet the target consumer's need(s) or problem(s) as stated in Question #3

Every investment request now arrived at headquarters with this new upfront section. At the time, the company did not have a head of consumer research. The industrial design teams that were spread across the globe generated all of the creative thinking and insight. Before the investment requests could go to finance, someone had to review the consumer insight page and say *yes*, or *no, please revise*. And, because these requests described new products–services or renovations, there was a concern about sending the investment requests by email. This meant sitting in a room for hours and sifting through dozens of investment requests, writing a daily report stating which requests were approved, and which were not, and why not. As the creators of the consumer insight section, we became accountable. In a major, global, durable goods organization, there are multiple investment requests generated every day.

We have no idea whether this approach is still in use. Did it work? People did comply. It did put the needs-based, occasion-driven segmentation in front of everyone's eyes. But, to our knowledge, it did not produce creative thinkers nor did it generate a culture conducive to creativity.

5. Ask "is this actionable?"

Paradox ideas can be provocative. Ensuring that they can gain traction within the organization can be a challenge. Articulating how these can be implemented is essential. Ideas or insights must be actionable. We must understand what we will be able to do with the idea or insight. Otherwise, these are nice to have; they make us feel creative; but they do not move the business forward.

Professor Theodore Levitt once said, "Ideas are useless unless used. The proof of their value is in their implementation. Until then, they are in limbo." Professor Levitt's view was that focusing solely on the creative concept without taking the responsibility for its implementation is irresponsible. Further, the person who generated the idea must be the one to take responsibility for it, turning it into an innovation.[166]

When you design research, it is necessary to ask for each question's answer, "What am I going to do with this information?" Generating answers that are not particularly actionable is a waste of corporate resources and respondent effort. Many times clients show us multi-million dollar pieces of research and say, "What do I do with this?" A large mid-America-based manufacturer of office furniture had worked with a very well known management consultant on a segmentation study. They had no idea what do with the analysis. It did not seem to point to any actions.

New ideas for products and services can face similar barriers. It is difficult for many to grasp the possibilities of something that is new. When you ask consumers what they want, they tell you about what they already know. They are not good at envisioning some future product. Ask people about dog food. They want a dog food their dogs will eat. This is not hard to create, as dogs seem to eat everything, including leather shoes. But, ask people about problems with dog food, and even today with all the dog food options, there are avenues for new ideas.

People love to complain. Focusing on solving problems with

relevant, differentiated products and services produces actionable ideas. At McDonald's, one of our first meetings concentrated on the development of a new chicken sandwich. Why? The answer was the climbing popularity of chicken over beef. A new chicken sandwich would bring in new customers. Was a new chicken sandwich solving a problem with our menu? No. The priority problem with the menu was that moms with kids found themselves sitting at a table with nothing to eat while their kids ate their Happy Meals. Rather than test a new chicken sandwich to bring in new customers, how about developing something for people who are already in the restaurant but not eating? This led to the Chicken Caesar Salad with Paul Newman salad dressing.

SMART HOME: BEING AHEAD OF TIME IN THE PRESENT

In 2000, we consulted to a joint venture project to help a group of engineers from a telecommunications company and a durable goods company with their idea for in-home connectivity and smart appliances. The two companies selected a team that soon rented amazing office space with fabulous furniture, and great views; logos and business cards; and, a fairly substantial budget.

The idea was visionary at the time: make products and technologies for the connected home with trouble-free access to household electronic services. The kitchen would become the center for all household management with intuitive appliances having electronic interfaces. This is one of those cases of the "pioneers are the ones with the arrows in their backs." As engineers, they understood the technology, the telecommunication issues, and they understood the problem-solution issues. They had the insight of making the interfaces and electronics personalized. But, the project stumbled at execution. The team could not move the ideas into action. They could not articulate what benefits consumers would have based on this particular product/service set. They could not settle on the types of services that would be best to offer: family-focused; household management; or timesaving? They had a vision but there was no Internet of Things mindset or reality. They saw something but could not breathe it into life. The saddest bit about the demise of this project is that today we see the smart home as relatively commonplace. But in 2000, the team was frustrated at their inability to move past vision into execution.

APPLE CANDY: MAKING A SOFT CARAMELIZED APPLE CANDY

We once worked with a food scientist who believed there was a huge market for a soft chewing, caramelized apple candy. He had a dream, and he wanted to bring it to life. At the time, the only apple candy you could buy was a hard taffy-coated apple on a stick, a parent's nightmare, and a dentist's opportunity. Our scientist envisioned an apple bar. Not exactly a Fig Newton type of soft candy but more of crunchy deliciously sweet, real apple, caramelized candy bar. He had worked for years in the food and confectionary business. He was the type of guy who could become lost in fabulous thought upon entering a test kitchen. The recipe was finally completed. Manufacturing was all ready. Distribution had been figured out. Packaging was being sent to the printer. Unfortunately, the chemistry of apple and its sugars, and the other ingredients turned the bar into such a glass-like coating that the model eating it for a commercial cut her gums and lips. The project came to a halt.

6. BE A RUNWAY NOT A CONTROL TOWER[167]

This phrase from a recent article in a Singapore newspaper is a great way to put a frequent occurrence: the opposition to change. As David Gauke, Chief Secretary of Treasury (United Kingdom) said in an interview on February 13, 2017, the idea is not to oppose change but to drive it. Branded Paradox Promises mean looking at your products and services in a different way. In our recent book, *Six Rules of Brand Revitalization, Second Edition*, we look at the problems with not changing; changing just for the sake of changing; sticking with the "basics;" and the benefits of institutionalizing change to create a change mindset, which makes the organization open to change. Here is some of what we said:

> "Brand teams need to be flexible. They need to be able to make changes when necessary. ….. Continuing to do the same old things when the world is different is a formula for failure. However, the biggest challenge is ensuring that the brand teams are open to change and the environment is conducive to change, if and when it comes."[168]

The company's culture sometimes is the control tower focusing on avoiding any and all risk. Brands flourish in supportive organizational cultures. Brands must stay relevant, and this requires change. If the organization is risk averse or closed to change, it creates an inflexible and relevancy-resistant environment. Certainly, eliminating silos and creating cross-functional teams help create a runway. But top management's verbal and visual approval is essential. The McDonald's 2002-2005 turnaround would not have happened without the strong support of Jim Cantalupo and Charlie Bell. These two leaders were proactive air traffic controllers who created a runway for the changes that had to occur. They not only listened but also advocated on behalf of brand initiatives that some rejected or stonewalled.

A seminal *Harvard Business Review* article in 2000 focused on the differences between the Theory E and Theory O schema of change. (See Endnotes for descriptions) The authors used Scott Paper led by "Chainsaw" Al Dunlop as an example of Theory E; and Andrew Sigler, Champion CEO as an example of Theory O. The authors point out, also, that in the fast-changing business world, embracing the paradox of both Theory E and Theory O led ASDA (the British-based, European supermarket retailer) to major success and sustained competitive advantage. They call it "managing the contradictions" necessary to achieve enduring profitable growth leveraging change.[169]

The Brand Academy: New Ideas and Business As Usual

Organizational education has many merits. It aligns employees around the culture and purpose of the company. It disseminates the values and language of the group. It imparts knowledge about the brands, and provides information, processes, and principles about a variety of subjects. At many companies, educational seminars and workshops are required. GE and Motorola are companies known for their vast, credible, educational options. We had the opportunity to create a program on branding for a client where most employees understood "brand" as a slogan, logo or an advertising campaign.

The participant take-away from this Brand Academy was always positive. People became energized. They believed that there would be a sea change in the company, and in their jobs. Aside from the required tools and templates, people gained knowledge and insight into how to create, nurture, grow, and lead powerful brands. They learned that how you run your brand is how you run your business. They had ideas about what they should and could do starting tomorrow.

And, then after the Brand Academy, they went back to their desks. Their managers would say, "Sounds as if this was a rewarding experience. Now, let's get back to work. We do not have time for any changes." The Brand Academy assessment questionnaires were an unfortunate look at how people deal with or do not deal with change. After three years of the Brand Academy, it became clear that the bottleneck was upper management: they were the control towers. The Brand Academy died a premature death.

Too Much Change: New is Usual

When organizations fall in love with a new book or a new management approach, and go through "re-orgs" with each of these romances, employees become inured to change. At one service company, the president changed every two years. The employees knew they could hold off on implementation of "disagreeable" actions because all they had to do was wait two years. This attitude became an impediment to moving forward, and the brand fell behind competitors. The managers became the control towers.

At another global services company, outside HR and management consultants were routinely hired to generate scenarios, global reorganizations, and strategic prioritizations. There could be two or three different "change streams" happening simultaneously. Each one of these initiatives required lengthy executive interviews; multiple presentation decks for the senior managers, for the C-suite; and special reports for the Board of Directors. Once approved, there were seminars and workshops with exercises, brochures, and big rollout events. People moved offices, and lost or gained new team members, and titles. When we arrived, there were two major corporate strategy initiatives, one HR initiative, and two brand rejuvenations to which we were assigned. In speaking with the brand leaders, it became clear that they absorbed all the disruptions, and knew that if they did not like scenario A, they could wait a couple of months. The acceptance of constant change made our projects easier and more difficult: easier because asking for alignment around a new approach generated immediate activity, with a "take that hill now" mind-set; more difficult because there was a group belief that we would go away soon.

7. FIGHT THE HYPNOSIS OF THE MEASUREMENT MYSTIQUE

In a world where marketing activities and budgets are squeezed by limited resources, there is a trend to over-rely on metrics to validate the value of marketing. Measurement has a role to play in marketing: in brand design, in package design, in innovation and renovation, in store design, in industrial design, in media assessment, satisfaction research, preference research, brand power, and in communications design. Unfortunately, as business has become more demanding, business has become more defensive. We allow the measurement to take over the role of marketing expertise, judgment and experience.

We constrain creativity by allowing measurement to throw out truly good ideas too soon. Here are two problems: 1) Measurement can provide direction for decision-making. But now, measurement is increasingly the decision-maker. 2) Measurement can guide creativity by providing an informed framework. But now, measurement compels creativity to conform.

Measurement should be a learning tool, not a rationalization tool. However, we allow ourselves to be mystified by the math of metrics. With metrics, statements both mean what they say and say what they mean. In other words, it is cut-and-dry not conceptual. And, the more complicated the methodology, the more credible the result.

We find ourselves managing the measurements. Secret, proprietary techniques, the proverbial, proprietary black box, rule the decision-making world. We defer decisions to mysterious measurement techniques. We make clear decisions based on unclear tools and techniques. Instead of transparency, we rely on mystery. We allow process to dictate over passion. We sacrifice accountability on the altar of measurement. Why? We fear failure. When our decisions fail, we say, "It is not my fault. The measurement processes made me do it."

Disciplined research is an important contributor to effective business management. Measurement can evaluate but not create ideas. As we have previously pointed out, creative ideas require creative insight. Real, actionable insight will not come from superior data analysis. Superior analysis provides understanding of where we are, and how we got to where we are. It does not provide insight into what kind of future we can create. Algorithms can make predictions but they cannot provide judgment. Marketers must use their expertise and their judgment and their creativity to make reasoned, informed, and insightful decisions. The researcher is as important as the research.

What is the role of measurement for paradoxes and Paradox Promises? One way to use metrics to the advantage of creativity is in new product development, where we can turn prioritized consumer insights into possible products or service concepts: identify the most promising concepts, develop further, evaluate further, and then identify the one(s) that are fit to bring into product development.

Testing plays a critical role. Unfortunately, most quantitative concept research is designed to assess winners and losers. We know what scored best. But, we do not know really "why" the concepts were rated as they did. Understanding "why" helps us to improve our thinking and our ideas. Understanding "why" can make a loser into a winner, and a winner even more appealing. Understanding "why" helps the truly creative breakthrough ideas make it through the screening filter. In other words, measurement should be an input into a marketing learning system, helping us to see opportunities to improve our ideas. Which are the ones to take forward? How can these be improved? We can use pure judgment, and some managers believe they have the skill and "gut feel" to make those choices. But, for most managers, informed, experienced judgment works best.

Effective marketing requires marketing discipline. The problem is we often seem to believe truths will appear out of a process or be revealed by a measurement system. We allow ourselves to believe that if we follow the steps, we will have discovered truth. This is nonsense. Hiding behind process and metrics is a safe way to manage. But, effective brand management is not always about selecting the safest option. People make decisions; processes do not. Managers make choices; metrics do not. Data do not speak; leaders do.

The 85% Rule: Change without Changing

In order to control offerings and stymie new ideas, a division chief created a threshold for testing any new product concept. Brand teams were encouraged to think of new ideas. Many creative concepts were developed. But before the division chief would even consider an idea, the concept had to score 85% or higher on a concept test of his design. It was a very high bar. Most ideas were abandoned. The division introduced no new products, and no renovations to existing products. The head of manufacturing was thrilled because he did not have to make any alterations to his manufacturing line, but the brand teams were disappointed. Innovation came to a halt.

How to Smile: Process and Personable

When a brand starts to slide, the downturn affects everyone internally as well as externally. Customers feel the difference. When McDonald's was in the doldrums in 2002, crewmembers' attitudes reflected the unhappiness of franchisees and corporate headquarters. Working at McDonald's became an embarrassment for some restaurant employees. An outcome was a slide in customer service at the front counter. Customers reported that crewmembers were not friendly: all the customers saw at ordering and payment was the top of someone's head; no one looked up and, if someone did, no one smiled. The people who oversaw employee training conducted research that revealed the key issue was crewmembers had to smile. Based on research and psychology, the team developed a checklist for smiling. The mystery shoppers and other in-store researchers were tasked with rating crewmembers on the checklist. This did not produce friendly, in-store experiences.

One Million Dollars a Customer: Make-Believe and Metrics

A company wanted to buy back its brand name in the United States. In order to estimate the value of the brand so it could generate an appropriate price, the company conducted market research. The brand had a very good image. It had been the brand of choice in its competitive set for decades. Its name was synonymous with its category in much the same way that Hoover is (in the United Kingdom and Canada), where "Hoovering" is another word for vacuuming, or Xerox in America, where "Xeroxing" is a word for copying. In a changing world, our client's brand had lost prestige, and potential customers saw it as an outdated, old-fashioned product.

The American equity firm that owned the brand name asked for a very large sum of money in the hundreds of millions of dollars. However, our client's consumer research confirmed that the brand's current target audience was 65 years old and older, with an entrenched loyalist group of 80 years old plus. Young category users knew the brand's name but were not interested in purchase.

The sample size of the "senior" loyalists was only 50 people. However, the buyer company was not deterred. It envisioned a snappier, modern, chic, and with-it version of the brand that would appeal to a younger audience. A very cogent presentation convinced the equity seller that it might be best to part with the brand. After viewing the consumer research results, a sale price of $50 million was agreed. It was joked, among some who were skeptical of the purchase, that the sale price was $1 million for each of the 80-year-old loyalists in the research.

8. Do not fall for the killer question

Paradox Promise solutions are going to be new. Hopefully, the solution you develop is something that has not been offered before. Yet for risk-averse leaders, this is a problem. To mitigate their risk aversion, they pose the killer question, the question that brings everything to a halt: "Who has done this before? Please give me an example of something just like this that has succeeded." How can you answer this? After all, if you have something new, it implies that it has never been done before.

In an article on multinational business enterprises, the former AB Volvo president, Pehr Gyllenhammar, said,

> "Business only wants what is brave and innovative as long as it does not imply risk.... Everything should be predictable. The establishment and the owners dislike the unforeseen. Then, spokesmen can talk in rather solemn words about risk-willingness,

entrepreneurship and drive. But when they see it they do not like it."[170]

The evidence for a paradox may not be numerical. The "viability" of the idea must be supported but it will mean tracking the train of thought and synthesis. Where did this idea come from? How do you know these are the appropriate contradictory problems and/or needs? On what evidence do you base this direction?

Industrial Problem Detection: Simple and Multi-faceted

An industrial company was searching for the best, most powerful brand promise. In order to generate valuable, actionable information, we conducted a global problem detection study. A problem detection study starts with customers identifying a vast number of problems within a category, and with a usage. (This particular study generated close to 800 problems.) The research then looks as which problems are important and frequently occurring. An important problem that happens infrequently may be annoying but may not be worth pursuing. A frequently occurring problem that no one cares about may also be one for some later actions. Those problems that are important and happen often are the ones to pursue.

Based on the problems that rose to the top, we saw that there was one dichotomy that appeared regardless of product type: simplicity and complexity. What customers said was, "If the product is too complex, I may make a mistake. But if it is too simple, things will not turn out well." "If the product is too complex, I will feel incompetent and defeated. But if it is too simple, it will not perform, and I will feel frustrated and angry."

Underlying the paradox of simplicity and complexity was another paradox: relief and unease. Think of relief and unease as dimensions of simplicity and complexity. Relief and Unease referred to needs like these: Make me feel capable; make me feel competent; help me make it a job well done; help me feel at ease doing this task. Additionally, customers wanted this particular product assortment to address needs similar to these: make me feel organized; make me feel relaxed; help relieve my frustration.

The research that included laddering (a way to generate functional, emotional and social benefits), reflected information and data from nine countries. The presentation underscored feelings that the top management and their families including the CEO's family actually felt. The synthesis of the research provided enough information and direction for the CEO to make a decision to move forward because it was a common sense insight that could drive industrial design.

Japanese Luxury Vehicle: Old is New

A Japanese luxury vehicle was at a disadvantage in its competitive set. It was at least 10 years past its original launch. Drivers and potential drivers were not quite sure what the brand stood for not only in terms of image but also in terms of driving experience. Top management questioned the brand's viability. In fact, the brand was really considered to be close to its demise: it had turned into a financial drain for the corporation. After extensive discussions with the global leaders of this brand, we tried an experiment with the brand team members who were determined to keep the brand alive.

The concept of "Japanese luxury" was problematic. Aside from Mikimoto pearls, no one had a definition of what this could be, and how to apply it to the brand. It had to be founded on satisfying a need, not just features-based. The features are the support for the benefits. But what were the benefits? What was the brand experience?

We conducted a Photosort exercise where the managers and brand leaders sorted a deck of photographs across several questions. At the end of the exercise, we looked at the results and were surprised by the consistency of the visual pattern, and the paradox visible in the cards. For example, there was an antique chair and an ultra modern chair; an old covered bridge and a Calatrava bridge; a wood-burning stove and an Aga range; a traditional Swiss watch and a Swatch watch; a Tiffany lamp and a modern IKEA hanging light; a thatch-roof cottage and a Frank Lloyd Wright glass house. What we saw was old and new: tradition wrapped in modernity, piety and performance, and vice versa. Working with the teams, we developed a way of explaining the brand's Japanese luxury in this context, creating a Paradox Promise, and a Paradox Promise dictionary. The designers in the group provided insight on how this idea could be brought to life in a clay model. The researchers went back to recent research to find support they may have overlooked. The group developed a brief to take to top managers, ending with the CEO giving the brand a reprise.

9. You can't hurry love[171]

Finding the paradox(es) may take a little time. There is a lot of information available, externally and internally. Search and synthesis require patience. These are iterative processes. With search, it means looking down all avenues in all directions before moving on. It means going back and forth over the same territory because sometimes you may miss something, so, go back in the opposite direction. You need to look things over; turn things over; dig around. It is a massive collection process across disciplines, geographies, and functions. For synthesis, the pattern recognition and the understanding of the outliers are critical. This is not an instant happening: there may be a Eureka moment but it is more a slow, logical unveiling in a non-linear way. Having said this, a time framework is a good thing to establish. Creative synthesizers like having a set of borders to work within, in this case a time frame.

McDonald's: Forever Young

When we joined McDonald's in September of 2002, the first task was to redefine a more current, relevant brand promise. The time frame was until November 2002, three months. The new idea had to be ready prior to the holiday season in order to present it internally, especially to the United States team in January 2003. It was doable;

it just took a great deal of coordination and collaboration. Studies from all 119 countries had to be sent in to Oak Brook, IL. We needed to review all of these studies, synthesize the information, and then, prioritize and group the information. The Brand Brief could not be created until the brand's promise and essence were articulated. There was a great sense of urgency. The share price and morale were at their lowest. Restaurant traffic was in steep decline. However, we recognized that we could not cut corners by skimming the information. There was intense pressure to deliver instantly. We found a room that hid behind the Boardroom. It had no phone, no windows, and a large table. We could shut out the clamor for an immediate answer. At the end, we not only had the insights to create Forever Young.

The Role of Culture: Big and Fast

Culture affects timing. A proactive, aligned organization can aim for something and achieve it. There are those who believe that big companies or brands are cautious and risk-averse. They believe that when you are big, you can be too slow to change and too slow to be creative. But that is not true. Technology has changed the landscape so big companies such as GE, IBM, Google, Amazon, and Ford, for example, are fast moving, innovative behemoths.

This belief that big is slow was prevalent at McDonald's in 2002, and was one of the major criticisms by outside observers. Critics said that it would be impossible to turn the Golden Arches battleship around quickly. What these critics missed was McDonald's is not a battleship: it is an armada of thousands of small speedboats manned by franchisees. Another thing the critics missed was the power of alignment around a very specific, very clear, focused goal, the revitalization of a brand everyone involved loved. And, third, the critics overlooked the core entrepreneurial culture that Ray Kroc instilled: it was very much alive.

But not every culture stays true to its founder's zeal or is able to become proactive. Culture is always the winner over strategy. A consensus-driven, risk-averse culture will spend time believing that if everyone were just a little bit more educated, great things will happen: continue to educate and eventually they will come to understand. Yet, understanding may not lead to action. And, all it takes is one regional leader or one division manager to say "No," and the project slows down, as another attempt at "educating" takes place. Companies such as this have enormous patience. Patience is not persistence. Patience means waiting it out. Persistence means continuing to go for something even in the face of resistance.

Summary

Nine Principles for Finding Paradoxes and Generating Paradox Promises

Identifying paradoxes and generating Paradox Promises require looking at information in different ways. It also requires a review of your enterprise to determine whether the right people are in place for the right tasks, and that the organization will support change. We provide nine principles for action.

1. Look for the little things: change the way you investigate
2. Look for ideas outside of your standard social media circles, favorite periodicals and journals: expand your knowledge horizon
3. Differentiate information from trends from insights: be clear as to what you are doing
4. There is no formula for creative thinking: create an organization that is open to creativity
5. Ask "is this actionable?": creative ideas are only ideas until implemented
6. Be a runway not a control tower: let the organization implement
7. Fight the hypnosis of the measurement mystique: use metrics to advance the efforts, not to stymie efforts

8. Do not fall for the killer question: know on what evidence your paradoxes rest
9. You can't hurry love: take the time to do this correctly but move expeditiously

PART 4

LESSONS FROM CREATING PARADOX PROMISES

Brands have implemented Paradox Promises over the years. Apple maximized computing and fun; Gore-Tex made fabric that is breathable and waterproof; The Franklin Mint created collectible art for the masses; Diet Coke offered great taste with no calories while Miller Lite had great taste that is less filling; Dawn dishwashing liquid promises hard on oil and grease but gentle enough to wash pollutants off of sea birds and animals.

Today, in The Age of I with the Collision of the forces of Globalizing, Localizing and Personalizing, Paradox Promises are even more important as drivers of brand success leading to enduring profitable growth.

Here are eleven lessons we learned while working with clients to identify paradoxes, and then, generate and implement Paradox Promises.

LESSONS

LESSON 1: IMPORTANCE OF THE PARADOX PROMISE

Although we have a chapter on the some of today's most noticeable contradictory needs that brands satisfy with maximized solutions, figure out what is best for your brand(s) by knowing your customers.

There are many different research techniques that are now in vogue for understanding customers. We will not enumerate these. However, all are based on discovering where are the best opportunities. At the heart of these techniques is the simple concept of solving problems. As we said above, people are pain avoidance mammals. Find the contradictory pain points and develop solutions.

We discussed how the frozen dairy desserts category is exploring the ways in which to address the paradox of wellness and indulgence: how do we communicate our inherent healthfulness while providing pleasurable extravagance? In other words, how to become a permissible pleasure? One idea posited in the discussion is the premium paradox. A dessert that eschews technological ingredients for the real, full fat, real sugar ingredients may seem more healthful.[172] Clean is associated with healthful (as Panera Bread explains) but it is also associated with handcrafted and artisanal. Using organic ingredients in an indulgent dessert can help sedate the feelings of guilt.

Take the dishwashing liquid paradox. Dishwashing liquid has to dissolve oil and grease with superior, tough cleaning leaving your dishes squeaky clean. Yet most people do not want their hands to be harmed by harsh chemicals. Dawn dishwashing liquid is tough on dishes but it is so gentle that wildlife rescue volunteers use it to cleanse animals that are caught in oil spills. If a baby duck or penguin covered in Dawn suds is cleaned so thoroughly that it waddles into the water to swim away, and is unharmed by a Dawn bath, my hands will be unharmed. The Dawn website has a section on saving wildlife and a section on fighting grease.[173]

In a sharing economy, there is the paradox of having something without owning it. We are less interested in owning something because owning comes with the burdens of commitment. We can rent things thereby having the brand experience without the problems of commitment. There is emotional difficulty involved in trade-off decisions: if there is too much concern, in this case, unwanted commitments that feel threatening, people will avoid making the decision. Brands such as Lyft, Rent-the-Runway, or BlaBlaCar in

Europe, address freedom from commitment anxieties: in other words, they help people avoid owner's remorse.

Renting is not just for consumer goods and services. Ashtead is a United Kingdom-based supplier of heavy-duty, construction equipment for hire. Interviewed in *Financial Times*, the CEO, Geoff Drabble said,

> "People just don't want to own stuff any longer." He added, "[Equipment rental] is the simplest business in the whole wide world. It's just, 'Make it easy, make it reliable, and make it affordable' – and why would you buy?"[174]

The solution to the paradox must be built into a total brand experience that is trusted and of value to the customer. This involves generating functional benefits, and emotional and social rewards. These must be defined in ways that the brand can own, and that are uniquely relevant, providing personalized immersion. Brand experiences, as defined by B. Joseph Pine II and James H. Gilmore in their seminal article, "Welcome to the Experience Economy," are memorable, personal, delivering sensations as well as functional benefits. The experiences they defined were staged to deliver education, escape, aesthetic and/or entertainment.[175]

Building a trustworthy, uniquely compelling total brand experience - maximizing a paradox - that is worth the cost is critical in today's marketing and business environment.

LESSON 2: IMPORTANCE OF FREEDOM WITHIN A FRAMEWORK

Brands need creativity and innovative thinking. This is how they stay relevant over time. But, it is not rampant creativity. Freedom within a Framework supports both the boundaries for creativity, and the environment where creativity grows. The Framework is not there to confine and control. It is there to care for, and cultivate great ideas.

It creates rules that do not rule out creativity. Within the Framework, there is freedom of creative thinking. This is the growing medium for borderless ideas. But without a framework there would be anarchy. So, within the framework, borderless ideas bump up against boundaries. There is abrasion. There is tension leading to original thinking. A brand has a vision and a promise. These must stay consistent over time and geography. These become the framework within which localizing and personalizing takes place. Marketing in today's world requires this paradox: it is your responsibility to be as freely creative and original as possible but stay within the framework.

At McDonald's (from 2002-2005), we created a brand framework. And, yet we also created Brand Journalism, a new marketing approach. Brand Journalism means telling the many facets of the brand story in a relevant way every day and everywhere the brand does business while staying true to the brand's framework. Brand Journalism was the chronicle of McDonald's.

Journalism is the collection and communication of news, events, and happenings. Journalism tells us what is going on in the world around us. Journalism informs, entertains, and persuades. Journalism lets the reader be a witness to history. It is the same with Brand Journalism. Brand Journalism is a chronicle of the varied things that happen in our brand world, throughout our day, throughout the years. A brand can mean different things to different people. It does not have one brand position. It is positioned differently in the minds of kids, teens, young adults, parents, or seniors. It is positioned differently at breakfast, lunch, dinner, snack, weekday, weekend, with kids, or on a business trip. No one communication alone tells the whole brand story. Each communication provides a different insight into our brand. But, because it keeps the integrity of the brand vision and promise, it all adds up to a coherent journalistic brand chronicle.

Freedom within a Framework ensures that the audacious and courageous thinking that every brand needs must be generated within its foundational framework so it does not detract from the brand's essential integrity.

LESSON 3: IMPORTANCE OF ORGANIZATIONAL DIVERSITY OF THINKING

Corporations put a great deal of effort into diversity programs and education. These are designed to produce a fair, safe, and representative workplace that is sensitive to different cultures, genders, and ethnicities. On the other hand, not enough effort is placed behind diverse ways of thinking. Many organizational cultures tend to hire those who fit in. There are benefits to this. A consensus-driven culture usually does not hire iconoclastic individuals. And, iconoclastic individuals may feel uncomfortable when they are forced to conform, or forced to struggle daily in breaking down barriers to new ideas and change. Cultures that are analytic tend not to want lateral thinkers. Creative cultures have trouble assimilating linear thinkers. If you are a technology-dependent company, it makes sense to hire people who are comfortable and expert with technology. If you are a financial company, it makes sense to hire those who know finance, spreadsheets, accounting, and so forth. In the 1990's, enterprises that wanted innovative ideas created "skunk works" crews that had separate offices and locations with teams that were not integrated into the mainstream of the business. IBM did this with the ThinkPad group. Today, some organizations, recognizing the need for creativity, hire consultants to educate employees into creativity.

We had an experience with an engineering company that saw an opportunity in making all its mid-level employees creative, inventive geniuses. The program was many months long; very expensive requiring time away from work; and, included mandatory sessions of "fun" activities. Instead of hiring creative design engineers, the company invested in changing the way its current engineer base thought. In essence, the company wanted its analytic thinkers to become lateral thinkers as well. It was not a happy ending. The final event marking the highpoint of internal imagination, ingenuity and inventiveness, focused on an exercise where teams presented their final projects: a new kind of toaster. This happened in the largest auditorium with as many employees as possible attending. A lot of senior executives were expecting James Dyson types of inventions. Instead, there was a less than stellar parade of toasters that did nothing to support an infusion of newly found creativity. The auditorium response was rather tepid. Rather than turning engineers into inventors, this organization might have spent the time hiring creative thinkers, and then, making sure the culture became conducive to creativity. At the end of the toaster exercise session, the new head of purchasing delivered a speech on how he would rationalize the excessive number of suppliers used by the organization. His 10-minute speech on procurement and audits received a standing ovation.

We have discussed the need for corporate diversity of thinking. Especially when there are cross-functional teams, making sure that the teams are ambidextrous is critical. Different perspectives allow for more creative, productive thoughts that lead to actions. Hiring for skills, as well as for diverse thinking, benefits brands and the businesses that own them. For example, synthesis is a skill that is essential to forming relevant, actionable information from reams of data. Synthesis creates ideas formed from reviewing different disciplines, generating something new from existing knowledge. We continually urge clients to hire brand people who may have skills outside of an MBA or a statistics background. Brands need lateral thinkers as well as linear thinkers. At McDonald's, Ray Kroc was the visionary founder, while Fred Turner was the disciplined organizer.

LESSON 4: IMPORTANCE OF COLLABORATION

New Brand Leadership focuses on an organizational mindset, structure and process for managing global brands: The Collaborative Three-Box Model.[176] The Collaborative Three-Box Model addresses the many challenges and obstacles inherent in global, multi-national and national marketing. Collaboration comes from Latin meaning "working together." In a highly fractionated business environment that has multiple offices, multiple functions and, sadly, multiple silos, sitting around a table to work together may be difficult and non-productive. Our view is that there is an old-think way of conducting brand management, and it is not viable in today's vibrant marketplaces. Our Collaborative Three-Box Model

> "... Engages global, regional, national, and local leadership, instilling a system-wide openness, forward-looking, active participation on behalf of the brand and its business."[177]

Without effective collaboration, there is no sharing across functions, geographies, and brands. People prefer not to share data and information as this means a loss of control. Learning from within the organization is cheaper than repeating studies and tactics that lead to the same answers. We worked with one global organization that conducted over 100 separate, and expensive, pieces of research on the same critical issue because none of the locales would share across borders. This same organization found itself with over fifty studies on physical activity and exercise where the countries held the reports close to the vest as if their compatriots in different regions were in fact the competition. This behavior is not only unproductive but also extremely costly in terms of time, effort and money. Ideally, corporations should encourage information sharing, as there is a Return on Global Learning (ROGL) that goes beyond the cost savings: ROGL helps an enterprise become a learning organization.

Without collaboration, the idea that the center is the repository of all intelligence will persist. In many organizations the tension between the center and the regions is intense and stultifying, with neither willing to take accountability. One regional team in a global business, upon adopting The Collaborative Three-Box Model was distraught to learn that the accountability it had continued to ask for was now theirs, and the team leader was shocked. He was not shocked that there was new regional responsibility, which elevated his role, but shocked because it would require actual actions with increased, better resources that would cost money to put in place. All of a sudden reality set in: while he received the job description he had wanted, he recognized that along with revised budgeting, he would now be accountable for results.

Without collaboration, silos remain. Silos are bad for brands and for business. Collaboration is essential for success in a world that is increasingly global, local and personal.

> "Silos are deleterious to brand health and for organizational health. They create all sorts of bad behaviors, such as hoarding, stopping the spread of ideas, internecine conflicts, and reinforcements of the status quo. Silos are for storage, not sharing. They reinforce lack of accountability for business results; it is always the other silo's fault."[178]

LESSON 5: IMPORTANCE OF DISCIPLINE

Undisciplined thought and action are very risky. By their very nature, paradoxes require a different way of looking at satisfying needs. It means holding two opposing thoughts in mind, and then figuring out how to best optimize these for customers. Rather than gambling with the future, base your strategies, movements, and tactics on a systematic, thoughtful, creative, disciplined decision-making process. When we worked with a fast food company that was in a crisis and needed an urgent turnaround, the center was launching new sandwiches and abandoning them instantly. Promoting these new entries stopped immediately when these failed to generate the numbers. We used to see this in the automotive industry. Launch and abandon is an undisciplined approach that leads to failure. Sometimes it will be launch now and tweak later: this is also undisciplined.

It is a paradox that when immediate action is needed it is good to have self-control. But, this is what having a framework will provide. It is also the guiding force behind a coherent Plan to Win. A Plan to Win is a one-page management strategy to gain alignment around all actions. It addresses the eight Ps: Purpose, Promise, People, Products (including services), Place, Price, Promotion, and Performance. The Plan to Win is the discipline that creates focus across all functions. Without a cohesive Plan to Win, actions seem to be purposeless, haphazard, and illogical. Actions appear to be thrown against the wall, waiting to see what will work. Inconsistent brand and business building can create internal chaos. A Plan to Win creates a common clarity that encourages everyone to aim in the same direction by having the same goals and priorities. You cannot be successful if you are unfocused. Create discipline.

Lesson 6: Importance of Strategic Dexterity

By strategic dexterity, we mean the ability to manage the strategic paradox of planning and flexibility. Yves Doz and Mikko Kosonen[179] describe this as having strategic agility, being able to create and implement prearranged, deliberate strategies while being open to and able to evolve when disruptions happen or business, environmental, political, geographic circumstances alter the landscape. In our book, *Six Rules of Brand Revitalization, Second Edition: Learn the Most Common Branding Mistakes and How to Avoid Them*,[180] we discuss several tendencies that lead enterprises to stay static rather than maximize deliberate and disruptive.

For example, being strategically insensitive means having a disregard for the changing world. It means that you do not have the insight to understand what possible changes may occur. Not paying attention to customers, their needs, their problems, or their beliefs, and values ensures that you are not current. It insulates you from innovation and renovation. It makes the assumption that what you always did will continue to work. To be strategically sensitive means having an informed grasp on the potential scenarios and areas for possible disruption.

Or there is the arrogance of success. Nothing fuels arrogance like triumph. We discussed the story of Kellogg: the company continued to hold onto the notion that consumers persist in arising every morning to have a bowl of sugared cereal. The world has changed. Even those eating at home have moved on to different sorts of breakfast foods.

One of the ways that brands (and the businesses that own them) wind up in strategic trouble is holding on to strategic plans that are calculated, calcified, and confirmed. There is no ability to bend for disturbances that break the boredom barrier. This reinforces tendencies for trouble such as: complacency, failure to innovate, lack of focus on the core customer, backtracking to basics, and lack of a coherent Plan to Win.[181]

Consumers are not able to tell you what the future will bring. Asking people to let you know what they want is a waste of time, as they will tell you what they already know. No one in the late 1980's said "I want a phone I can keep in my pocket that takes pictures, does my banking, lets me watch TV, allows me to text, and sends email."

Strategic dexterity allows brands to be resolute and responsive, disciplined and dexterous, at the same time. It is a core business concept for the paradoxical Age of I.

Lesson 7: Importance of Marketing

There is no question that marketing has done itself a great disservice over the past decades. Marketing has fallen in love with the increasing number of communication channel opportunities: social media, mobile everything, streaming anything, entertainment, events, online, swiping, digital, and so on. But, communications channel management is not marketing management. This fractionalization of functions is fracturing the role of marketing. Our love affair with technology, and the digitalization of our lives has led to marketing that is sliced, diced, spliced, strangled, and mangled by specialists competing with each other for limited corporate resources.

This fractionalization is demeaning the role of the Chief Marketing Officer (CMO). The CMO's role is often reduced to managing this competition and attempting to force co-operation. The CMO has become a ringmaster juggling the different "acts" that want to communicate with the audiences. We have managed to marginalize marketing while trivializing the role of the CMO, turning this crucial position into coordinator, mediator, and arbitrator in Chief. The fractionalization of marketing has changed the perception of marketing into a trade not a profession. The marketing department is seen as the place where ads are made, slogans are sung, logos are designed, and frivolous expenditures are rampant.

Marketing is about managing the business and managing the business is bigger than managing messages and media. Peter Drucker, the most respected management guru ever, once said, "The purpose of business is to create a customer."

Effective marketing is not merely about message and media management; it is about business management. It is fundamentally about attracting and retaining customers. The purpose of brand management is the enduring profitable growth of the business. The purpose of the business plan is the enduring profitable growth of the brand. Interestingly, marketing has inherent tensions, paradoxes that need optimizing but unfortunately fall prey to either/or: efficiency OR effectiveness, marketing OR shareholder value, brand equity OR customer equity (customer lifetime value), short-term OR long-term, reach OR frequency, quantity of sales OR quantity of sales. In the Paradox Planet, management must optimize these tensions, not choose between them.

Marketing should be evaluated on its ability to make strategic investments that promise returns greater than their costs.[182] But, this is not the case. Finding the paradox and creating, then implementing the Paradox Promise is essential, and yet the functions necessary for these strategic activities are always those that take the direct cost-management hit. This is because it is always easier to measure the costs than the effects. To be successful with paradoxes and Paradox Promises, restore relevance and importance to marketing.

LESSON 8: IMPORTANCE OF STANDING UP FOR WHAT YOU STAND FOR

Increasingly, people look to brands and business for behaviors that sync with their own values. As we see in the paradox of **Improve Me and Improve We**, there is a desire to connect with, and purchase from brands and businesses that are actively involved in making things better on a global, local, and personal basis. People are aware of those enterprises that talk and do not act. There is no place to hide in our open-information-now world. Saying you have a program that is only for your own employees is great for the employees but how does that affect the greater good and me? Saying one thing, and not delivering, or delivering on something else, also does not make the grade.

The women's athletic clothing brand, Athleta, has its sustainability commitment on the first page of its catalogue suggesting to readers that they should learn more on the website. The Athleta commitment addresses sustainability for the planet and for the components of its products, women's issues, and their Athleta employees. It is committed to Fair Trade and certifies its apparel, "which gives a premium to the factory workers (mostly women), increasing earnings, improving their livelihood and that of their communities." Additionally, Athleta participates in the PACE program (a Gap Inc. initiative) that "provides life skills education to the women who make the clothes."[183]

Athleta's focus on its employees' well being is a critical current evolution of CSR. The evolution of Social Responsibility from being green to being good means that there are many opportunities for matching the brand/business with its values and an area of interest. In a November 18, 2016, interview on *Bloomberg TV*, a British Lord (an economist) discussed the fact that Brand-Business Social Responsibility is no longer just about the environment, and giving back to communities. He felt that Social Responsibility in today's environment must focus on the behavior of brand-business job creation, and training/re-training people for new jobs.

If you think corporate social responsibility (or brand social responsibility) is tangential, read the news reports from February 20, 2017, on the Kraft Heinz withdrawal of its Unilever takeover bid.

A priority at Unilever is its decades old commitment to sustainability. Unilever has "The Unilever Sustainable Living Plan" with its own website. On the website, Unilever states the Plan as a, "blueprint for achieving our vision to grow our business, whilst decoupling our environmental footprint from our growth and increasing our positive social impact." It speaks to Unilever's desire to manage how it sources its materials and intends to further its sustainability goals; the company seeks to "partner with others in business, government and society." The statement ends with this:

> "Faced with the challenge of climate change and the need for human development, we want to move towards a world where everyone can live well and within the natural limits of the planet. That's why our purpose is 'to make sustainable living commonplace'."[184]

Kraft Heinz is managed according to a philosophy of extreme cost cutting, with little or no resources for organic growth, which could have created a major tension if the companies combined.[185] Whether this defining CSR commitment was a high priority for the withdrawal or not is not the issue. The issue is how important to Unilever its commitments are, and how these commitments are an ingrained part of its value system, while imbuing its products and its footprint in the local markets in which it competes.

Whole Foods Market® is another example of values-based commitment that permeates the entire enterprise from its workers wellbeing to the welfare of the people, plants, dairy, animals, fish, and fowl that wind up on the shelves, and in the fresh sections, and freezer cases. A visit to their website informs you that, "Values Matter - At Whole Foods Market®, 'healthy' means a whole lot more. It goes beyond good for you, to also encompass the greater good. Whether you're hungry for better, or simply food-curious, we offer a place for you to shop where value is inseparable from values."[186] Whole Foods has an extensive list of beliefs across many different issues. And, it has numerous personal values as well as commitments to a wide range of societal forces. The sense of goodness for planet, people and animals as well as fish and fowl is palpable.

Chipotle's founder Steve Ells believes that fast food need not be terrible for you: it is not how fast the food is made; it is how good or bad the food is for you. Chipotle grew on the basis of its commitment to Food With Integrity. Integrity means honesty, honor, morals, ethics, probity, decency, truthfulness and trustworthiness, just to give a sample of synonyms. When faced with a series of e coli outbreaks, Chipotle's spokesperson, Chris Arnold, announced that now the enterprise would focus even more on food safety. One would assume that integrity encompasses an ethical code to keep customers from falling ill. Keeping customers safe is the decent, moral, honorable thing to do.

Finding the paradox(es) that works for you and then developing and implementing the Paradox Promise should happen within the context of your values. A disconnect between brand-business and internal values is potentially and profitably harmful. Stand up for what you stand for by creating a visible, vocal and active context for your beliefs.

Lesson 9: Importance of Internal Marketing

Organizational alignment and commitment behind the Paradox Promise(s) are necessary for attainment of your goals. After Purpose and Promise, and before Performance, there is the Five Action Ps section of the Plan to Win: People, Product (including service), Place, Price, and Promotion. These are in order of priority. "People" is first because if you put the outside world ahead of your own people, you will not be as successful. Employees must come first. This requires internal marketing. Without internal marketing, you run the risk of acquiescence over adherence.

We spoke about the need for a revitalized marketing function above. But that external marketing will be for naught if the internal audience is disconnected from the action and unaware of why what you are doing is important. To bring the Paradox Promises to life across geography and functions, you need people to believe in not belittle the direction.

Internal Marketing has four parts[187] that continue to strengthen each other: in other words, Internal Marketing is an ongoing process. The four parts are Education, Implementation, Inspiration, and Evaluation. Together these create a virtuous circle of behavior and attitude reinforcement.

1. Education: What are we doing? Why are we doing it? Why now? What does this mean to the enterprise/brand?
2. Implementation: What does this all mean to me? What am I going to have to do differently? What will the enterprise/brand have to do differently? What support will be provided?
3. Inspiration: Why should I believe? Is leadership truly committed? Are management behaviors in sync with The Plan to Win? What kind of future do we wish to create?
4. Evaluation: How will we measure and manage progress? How will we measure and reward those who produce the right results in the right way? Will we learn from failure or punish?

In any organization, people need to know what is expected of them, and on what basis they will be evaluated and compensated. From our perspective the rules of Internal Marketing are 1) inform everybody and keep them informed; 2) define success so that everyone knows what the winning hand looks like; 3) provide educational opportunities so everyone can perform to expectations and experience attitude change; 4) recognize and reward genuine progress by always celebrating the small successes. Provide feedback and incentives to move forward; and 5) focus on continuous improvement.

LESSON 10: IMPORTANCE OF TRUST

We began by discussing the uncertainty, anxiety and anger that permeates today's world. These have taken a toll on institutional trust. Over the years, we have written about trust and how critical it is not just for interpersonal relationships, but also for all relationships, including business and brand. Trust is the focus of sociologists, anthropologists, academics, psychologists, politicians, and pollsters. Every year, Edelman, the respected public relations firm, delivers another *Trust Barometer*. And, the decline in institutional trust is significant.

Trust affects loyalty. It has a huge influence on a whether to commit to a relationship. There are many definitions of trust, and we have one as well: "the confidence you have relying on the brand to live up to its promises and its reputation of authority based on leadership, credibility, integrity, and responsibility."[188]

Social psychology supports the point that credibility or expertise will not matter if there is no trust. Brand trust significantly affects consumer commitment. This influences price tolerance. Brand trust is a critical piece of the decision process. If you want a strong, enduring, loyal relationship with a customer, the reams of marketing, social and psychological data, and research are clear: you must have brand trust. Trust is essential to the calculative process of brand acceptance.

In our work for the *IHG 2015 Trends Report* (available online at the IHG plc. website), we proposed that along with Financial Capital, Intellectual Capital, and Human Capital, organizations must add Trust Capital.[189] We define Trust Capital as the customer confidence in the authority, credibility, integrity, leadership, and responsibility of an organization to deliver promises of value to stakeholders. Trust Capital is a very important form of organizational wealth: it creates value. Accumulate Trust Capital in your trust bank so that it is available during a crisis or troubling times. As we say,

"Creating Trust Capital allows a brand (enterprise) to generate a trust reserve that helps through crises of brand (enterprise) character. A trust reserve of Trust Capital builds strong relationships over time."[190]

LESSON 11: IMPORTANCE OF TRUSTWORTHY BRAND VALUE™

The Paradox Promise creates the brand's (enterprise's) total brand experience. A brand's total brand experience is inexorably tied up with the customer's perception of the brand's trustworthy brand value. Over the years, the definition of the customer's perceived value equation evolved. For years, marketing focused on features and functions for the money. For example, on an old game show from the 1950's, *The Price is Right*, the host, Bill Cullen, described the show's offerings in terms of features and simple functional benefits.

> This brand new refrigerator has a side-by-side freezer!
> There are special drawers for keeping lettuce crisp!
> A special compartment keeps meat fresh!
> There are shelves on the inside of the door!
> And, yes… it comes in avocado green!

Marketing evolved to reflect the fact that people do not buy features, they buy benefits. As Theodore Levitt said in the famous 1960 *HBR* article, "marketing concentrates on the needs of the buyer."[191]

But, something else happened: we experienced the Sixties with its iconic Summer of Love. The Sixties gave us permission to not only focus on functional needs but also on the emotional need to feel good, really good, about ourselves. The Sixties gave us the permission to make choices based on emotional rewards. The customer perceived value equation was now more than just features and functions. Emotional rewards were also relevant. The value equation was changed forever.

In the 1980's, with the proliferation of two income families, YUPPIES, and the beginning of busy lives, price was no longer the only cost that people considered when evaluating value. Time was as precious as money, and, as we explained, our language reflects this. Do I really have to visit five car dealerships to find the best value for me when I can visit a single multi-brand dealer? The denominator of the value equation evolved to include both money and time.

By the turn of the 21st Century, there was again another evolution in customer perceived value. In addition to money and time, consumers added a third cost: effort. As our world became more technological and digital, with an explosion of choice, our expectations changed. We started assessing a brand's worth based on functional benefits and emotional rewards relative to money, time, and effort, where effort means the physical and mental energy cost. For example, I could have all the time in the world, but I stand dazed and confused in front of the granola bar section of the supermarket. To make the right choice, I must review and compare ingredients, nutritional components, RDA, fats, sugars, flavors, natural versus organic, brand name, reputation, and, of course, number of bars by size for the money. This takes a lot of exhausting mental effort that just happens to take a lot of time. Is it worth the effort?

The value equation continues to evolve. Some have dubbed our new world a shared experience economy. Consumers now look at the numerator of the value equation as a total brand experience defined in terms of functions, emotional *and* social benefits. Social benefits are not just about sharing and belonging, but also include the image this brand conveys about me, as well as the status and respect this brand confers on me. Consumers assess a brand's worth based on the total brand experience (functional benefits, emotional and social rewards) relative to the costs of money, time and effort.

But, there is a very important new component to the equation. It is a value multiplier, and that multiplier is trust. Trust is the consumer's belief that the brand will deliver the brand's total experience relative to the total costs. The new mental model of value is total brand experience relative to total experience costs all multiplied by trust. We call this the new Trustworthy Brand Value™ equation. Trust is the consumer's evaluation of future experience with the brand: How confident am I that this brand will deliver this experience for these costs?

If trust in the brand is high, then as a multiplier, the perceived brand value is increased. If trust in the brand is low, then the perceived brand value is decreased. If there is no trust in the brand, if trust in the brand is zero, then it does not matter what the promised brand experience is relative to the costs: anything multiplied by zero is zero.

Summary

There are eleven lessons to keep in mind when committing to and organizing for the discovery of paradoxes, and the delivery of Paradox Promises. Along with the principles in Part 3, these lessons help create a roadmap for enduring profitable growth.

1. Importance of the Paradox Promise
2. Importance of Freedom within a Framework
3. Importance of Organizational Diversity of Thinking
4. Importance of Collaboration
5. Importance of Discipline
6. Importance of Strategic Diversity
7. Importance of Marketing
8. Importance of Standing Up for what You Stand For
9. Importance of Internal Marketing
10. Importance of Trust
11. Importance of Trustworthy Brand Value™

CONCLUSION

We live in an uncertain changing world. Paradoxes are an outcome of uncertainty. But, these do not need to be negatives. In this unclear, tentative, volatile environment, difficult choices seem more challenging. Making a trade-off requires too much personal justification for not enough benefit. Rather than having to choose or accept a lesser solution, today we seek the maximization of contrary needs. Optimizing the contradictory sides of the paradox into a relevant, differentiated, trustworthy Paradox Promise is an opportunity for brands and business. Welcome to the Paradox Planet.

There are two major influences that have created and continue to create this situation, 1) The Age of I, and, 2) The Collision of Globalizing, Localizing and Personalizing.

"The Age of I" is the overarching dichotomy of today's society. Beyond the divisions of "haves" *and* "have nots" or "developed world" *and* " emerging countries," The Age of I refers to the tension between the need to belong (inclusivity) and the need to have a unique identity (individualism). It is an overarching paradox that drives our attitudes and behaviors. People want to be seen and respected as individuals with special characteristics, but also people want to belong to something bigger: a community, a network, a business, a family, an ethnic group, a religious institution, a union, or a nation. We want to be independent and interdependent at the same time.

The Age of I is not the only influence. The Collision of Globalizing, Localizing and Personalizing is another, equally vigorous influence that is affecting our world. Institutions, industries, societies, nations, brands, and business operate in a world where there are global needs, local needs, and personal needs that must be satisfied at the same time.

Finding paradoxes, and developing, then implementing Paradox Promises is not a panacea. It is a powerful approach to addressing the needs of a world where people prefer to not make trade-offs. Forcing people to make disagreeable choices or default choices can lead to complacency or grow into anger. "Good enough" does not lead to loyalty. The Paradox Promise does not mean you can have it all, nor does it mean that you are receiving a little bit of everything: it means in this choice situation, you can have the best of both.

Succeeding in The Paradox Planet has many challenges. This book provides ways in which you can manage with these challenges in order to make the paradoxes work for you, your brand, and/or your business.

ENDNOTES

Introduction

1. *Network* by Paddy Chayefsky. Copyright © 1976 Metro Goldwyn-Mayer Inc. and United Artists Corporation.
2. Itzkoff, Dave, *Mad As Hell: The Making of Network and the Fateful Vision of the Angriest Man in the Movies,*" Ties Books, Henry Holt and Company LLC, New York, NY, 2014.
3. Easterbrook, Gregg, "When Did Optimism Become Uncool?" *The New York Times*, May 15, 2016.
4. See book review in *The Economist*, "Enlightenment and its discontents: The roots of modern resentment," January 28, 2017: *Age of Anger: A History of the Present,*" by Pankaj Misha, Farrar, Strauss and Giroux, 2017.
5. Lewis, Helen, "Social media skew our memories in strange ways," *Financial Times*, February 21, 2017.
6. Jacobs, Emma, "Fear and trembling in the digital age, *Notebook, The Financial Times*, February 17, 2017.
7. Brooks, David, "The Movement Mentality," *The New York Times*, January 3, 2016; "One Community at a Time," *The New York Times*, May 17, 2016; and "The Fragmented Society," *The New York Times*, May 20, 2016.

Part 1: The Paradox Planet

8. Walsh, Kenneth T, "After Election Bitter Polarization Will Remain," *USNews.com*, November 4, 2016, www.usnews.com. And, West, Ed, "As the world gets wealthier we get more divided, *London Evening Standard*, November 16, 2016, www.standard.co.uk. Wong, Datuk Steven, "Let us not fall for 'post-truth' politics," *New Straits Times (Malaysia)*, January 3, 2017.

9. www.edelman.com/insights/intellectual-property/2016 - edelman-trust-barometer/
10. *Bloomberg*, "WEF Davos Panel on The Crisis of the Middle Class," January 18, 2017, http://www.bloomberg.com.
11. Wolf, Martin, "The losers are in revolt against the elites," *Financial Times*, January 27, 2016; see also, Rachman, Gideon, "World Economic Forum. Uncertain Future. Shadow of populism hangs over Davos: Delegates ponder possible Trump presidency, UK-EU spilt and borders clampdown," *Financial Times*, January 23-24, 2016; and Skapinker, Michael, "Davos CEO elite misjudges both its fame and its legitimacy, *Financial Times*, January 21, 2016.
12. The Futures Company, *Global Monitor 2013*.
13. Lewis, Martine W.; Andriopoulos, Constantine; Smith, Wendy K., "Paradoxical Leadership to Enable Strategic Agility," *California Management Review*, Vol. 50, No. 3, Spring 2014.
14. Collins, James C and Porras, Jerry I., *Built To Last: Successful Habits of Visionary Companies*, HarperCollins, New York, 1994.
15. Jahanmir, Sara F., "Paradoxes or trade-offs of entrepreneurship: Exploratory insights from the Cambridge eco-system," *Journal of Business Research*, Vol. 69, 2016.
16. For a brief discussion of decision-making see Frank R. Kardes, *Consumer Behavior and Managerial Decision Making*, Addison-Wesley Educational publishing, Inc., 1999, 144-151.
17. For a thorough review, see the monograph: Luce, Mary Frances; Bettman, James R.; and Payne, John W., "Emotional Decisions: Trade Off Difficulty and Coping in Consumer Choice," *Monographs of The Journal of Consumer Research*, ed. Deborah Roedder John, No. 1, University of Chicago Press, 2001.
18. Moon, Jang Ho and Sung, Yongjun, "Individuality within the group: testing the optimal distinctiveness principle through brand consumption," *Social Behavior and Personality: an International Journal*, January 1, 2015, Vol. 43, No. 1, 15.
19. Voyer, Benjamin C.; Kastanakis, Minas N.; and Rhode, Ann Kristin, "Co-creating stakeholder and brand identities: a cross-cultural consumer perspective," *Journal of Business Research*, Vol. 70, 2017, 399-410.
20. Fisher, Michael; Boland Jr., Roland; and Lyytinen, Kalle, "Social networking as the production and consumption of a self," *Information and Organization*, Vo., 26, 2016, 131-145.

21. Black, Ian and Veloutsou, Cleopatra, "*Journal of Business Research*, 2017, 416-429.
22. Bernstein, Jacob, "My Headphones, My Self," *The New York Times*, December 11, 2016.
23. Mims, Christopher, "Teens Use Video Chat to Hang Out," *The Wall Street Journal*, February 21, 2017.
24. Pareles, Jon, "Finding Festival Joy, Communally: Notable acts from this year's South by Southwest," *The New York Times*, March 20, 2017.
25. https://www.wework.com/mission
26. Luce, Edward, "Dreaming small: Is America losing the restlessness of spirit that once powered its economy? Edward Luce draws Toquevillian lessons from Tyler Cowen's latest critique," *Financial Times*, February 18-19, 2017; and Cowen, Tyler, *The Competent Class: The Self-Defeating Quest for the American Dream*, St. Martin's Press, 2017.
27. Hine, Thomas, *The Great Funk: Falling Apart and Coming Together (on a shag rug) in the Seventies*, Sarah Crichton Books (Farrar, Strauss and Giroux), NY, 2007.
28. Light, Larry and Kiddon, Joan, *New Brand Leadership: Managing at the Intersection of Globalization, Localization and Personalization*, Pearson Education, Old Tappan, New Jersey, 2015, p. 44.
29. Miller, Richard, *Bohemia: The Protoculture Then and Now*, Nelson-Hall, December, 1977.
30. Op.cit., Bernstein, December 11, 2016.
31. As quoted in Brooks, David, "How Covenants Make Us Stronger," *The New York Times*, April 5, 2016.
32. 2015 IHG Trends Report, *Building Trust Capital: The New Business Imperative in The Kinship Economy*, IHG, 2014.
33. Lovett, Ian, "The Benedict Option: Longing to lead more religious lives – and wary of the wider culture – a growing number of traditional Christians are creating their own small communities," *The Wall Street Journal*, February 18-19, 2017.
34. O'Connor, Sarah, "The highs and lows of hipster capitalism," *Financial Times*, January 11, 2017.
35. Publix supermarkets are located in seven states in the southeast United States from Virginia down through Florida.
36. Op. cit., Light, Larry, and Kiddon, Joan, 2015.
37. *The Economist*, "The retreat of the global company: the biggest business idea of the past three decades is in deep trouble," January 28, 2017.
38. Ibid., *The Economist*, January 28, 2017.

39. Yen, Dorothy Ai-wan, and Abosag, Ibrahim, "Localization in China: How *guanxi* moderates Sino-US business relationships," *Journal of Business Research*, Vol. 69, 2016, 5724-5734.
40. Clinique Laboratories LLC, advertisement for Clinique BIY™ Blend It Yourself Pigment Drops, *The New York Times Style Magazine,* 2017.
41. Shoemaker, Paul J. H., "The Future Challenges of Business: Rethinking Management Education," *California Management Review*, Vol. 50, No. 2, Spring 2008, 121.

PART 2: THE PARADOX PLANET'S PARADOXES

42. Club Med advertising supplement to *The New York Times Style Magazine*, February 14, 2016.
43. Rubin, Alissa J., "'Right to Disconnect' From Work Email and Other Laws Go Into Effect in France," *The New York Times*, January 3, 2017.
44. Huet, Ellen, "Camp Grounded: Where People Pay $570 To Have Their Smartphones Taken Away From Them," *Forbes*, June 20, 2014. And, Haber, Matt, "A Trip to Camp to Break a Tech Addiction," *The New York Times*, July 5, 2013.
45. http://digitaldetox.org
46. Sullivan, Andrew, "I Used To Be Human," *New York*, September 18, 2016.
47. Paul, Pamela, "Every Day's a Holiday (or Two)," *The New York Times*, April 17, 2017.
48. See Bachman, Rachel, "The New Gym Class, Live On Your Phone," *The Wall Street Journal*, January 23, 2017.
49. "Kuchler, Hannah, "Chatbot life beyond the grave," *Financial Times*, April 20, 2016.
50. Cohen, Roger, "Smartphone Era Politics," *The New York Times*, February 23, 2016.
51. *New York*, "Approval matrix," January 23-February 5, 2017.
52. Dugan, Conor, "The Personal Touch," *The Dartmouth*, January 31, 2017.
53. Koblin, John, "TVs Answer to Dark Days: NBC's 'This is Us' Proves Networks Can Still Make Hits, Even in Tumultuous Times," *The New York Times*, February 6, 2017.
54. *The Futurist*, December 2006.
55. Kerns, Jeff, "4 Control Trends that You Can't Ignore," *Machine Design* (Penton), February 3, 2017.
56. Porter, Charlie, "Nike's new moves," *Financial Times*, March 26-27, 2016.

57 Ellison, Jo, "Karl Lagerfeld on the crisis in luxury: Italians say slow down to fast fashion," *Financial Times*, February 26, 2016.
58 Ibid., Ellison, February 20, 2016.
59 Freda Salvador emails, January 23 and 24, 2017, www.fredasalvador.com.
60 Knothe, Alli, "Tesla Loyalty, Sight Unseen," *Tampa Bay Times*, April 1, 2016; and, Howard, Bill, "Now You Can Lease a Tesla Model S For Less While Waiting For Your Model 3," *EXTREMETECH.com*, August 23, 2016, https://www.extremetech.com.
61 Huyghe, Elke, Verstraeten, Julie, Geuens, Maggie and Van Kerckove, Anneleen, "Clicks as a Healthy Alternative to Bricks: How Online Grocery Shopping Reduces Vice Purchases," *Journal of Marketing Research*, February 2017, 61.
62 http://www.cadillac.com/world-of-cadillac/craftsmanship.html.
63 http://www.levi.com/US/en_US/features/madeandcrafted.
64 http://www.gq.com/story/new-classic-cars
65 Garfield, Simon, "Has tech ruined our relationship with time?: Simon Garfield explores our ambivalent attitude to the clock in the 21st century," *The Daily Telegraph* (London), October 1, 2016 Edition 1; National Edition.
66 Newman, Judith, "Getting Hygge with it: tips on how to relax, cuddle, sip cocoa, bake pastries, knit sweaters and above all – drink coffee," *The New York Times*, February 26, 2017.
67 Ferdman, Roberto A., "History of tea in the UK: How Britain fell out of love with its national drink: Google has honoured the UK's favourite drink with its own doodle. It is the most quintessential of beverages and everyone in the country drinks it, right? Wrong. It turns out the decades have turned a growing number of British people against their national pastime," *The Independent* (United Kingdom), September 23, 2016.
68 Stein, Sadie, "Copy That," Sign of the Times, *The New York Times Style Magazine,* February 19, 2017.
69 Thomas-Corr, Johanna, "Enter the now age: In Los Angeles, hippie crystals are being repolished and repackaged as the most chic of talismans," *Financial Times*, February 18-19, 2017.
70 Muhlke, Christine, "The Hippies Have Won," *The New York Times*, April 4, 2017.
71 *New Oxford American Dictionary*, Apple Mac Air.
72 Kapferer, Jean-Noël, "The Future of Luxury: challenges and opportunities," *Journal of Brand Management*, December 1, 2014, Vol. 21, No. 9, pp. 716-728.
73 DePillis, Lydia, "Coach 22: Exclusivity or ubiquity?" *Washingtonpost.com*, October 27, 2013, www.washingtonpost.com.

74 Ibid., www.washingtonpost.com, October 27, 2013.
75 *Shenzhen Daily*, "Coach 22: Can a handbag be 'luxury' if everyone owns one?" December 12, 2013.
76 Prokopec, Sonja, "Mass luxury: an oxymoron?; Nowadays, luxe brands are walking a fine line between exclusivity and attracting new business," *The Business Times Singapore*, April 5, 2014.
77 Shapiro, Nicole, "Premium brands just keep on walking: Be brave, exclusive ... assured of a high-quality product but be critical of the 'volume versus value' equation," *The Star (South Africa)*, January 9, 2016.
78 www.mindwhirl.com.
79 www.bringonthebeer.com.
80 Bernstein, Joshua M., "11 Hour Lines for a New Ale? Fans Wait, Breweries Worry," *The New York Times*, February 6, 2017.
81 Mobley, Esther, "The next obsession: California's new generation of must-have wine is not elite but still exclusive – a new generation of sought-after wines," *San Francisco Chronicle*, May 1, 2016.
82 *The Economist*, "How HoJo lost its mojo: The last outpost of a once-great restaurant chain is for sale," February 18, 2017, 25.
83 Cook, Everett, "The Last Howard Johnson's in the Universe: America's first great restaurant chain comes to the end of the road," *eater.com*, February 14, 2017, https://www.eater.com/2017/2/14/14601970/last-howard-johnson's-lake-george-new-york.
84 Baker, Todd H., "Where SoFi-Zenbanx merger falls short," *American Banker*, February 6, 2017, Vol. 1, No.24.
85 Wack, Kevin and Wisniewski, Mary, "SoFi-Zenbanx deal accelerates fintech convergence trend," *American Banker*, February 2, 2017, Vol. 1, No. 22.
86 Colvin, Geoff, "Knowing the Limits of Machines: Some Jobs Really Must Be Automated. Others Need The Human Touch. Which are Which? That's Your Call," *Fortune*, July 1, 2016.
87 *Entertainment Close-Up*, "HGS: Top 10 CX Trends In Customer Support for 2017," March 7, 2017, closeupmedia.com.
88 Thornhill, John, "Lunch with the FT Daniel Dennet: 'Don't kid yourself that robots are colleagues,'" *Financial Times*, March 4-5, 2017; and Thornhill, John, "Artificial intelligence is running wild while humans dither," *Financial Times*, March 7, 2017.
89 Wayne, Teddy, "Holdouts of the Social Media Age," *The New York Times*, March 27, 2016.
90 Jai, Tun-Min (Catherine) and King, Nancy J., "Privacy versus Reward: Do loyalty programs increase consumers' willingness to share personal

information with third-party advertisers and data brokers?" *Journal of Retailing and Consumer Services,* 2016, Vol. 28, 296-303.

91 Wittes, Benjamin and Kohse, Emma, "Empirical Data on the Privacy Paradox," *Lawfare,* January 17, 2017.

92 *Benzinga,* "Consumers increasingly aware of online security risks, but hold businesses responsible for data breaches, finds Gemalto study," January 17, 2017.

93 Bode, Karl, "Another Lawsuit Highlights How Many 'Smart' Toys Violate Privacy, Aren't Secure," *techdirt,* December 8, 2016, www.techdirt.com/articles.

94 Forrest, Conner, "IoT connected teddy bear leaks millions of kids' conversations, exposed database to blame," http://www.techrepublic.com/article/iot-connected-teddy-bear-leaks-millions-of-kids-conversations-exposed-database-to-blame/, February 28, 2017.

95 Thomas, Andrea, "German officials Order Parents to Execute a Spy – Cayla the Doll," *The Wall Street Journal,* April 14, 2017.

96 Hook, Leslie, "Privacy concerns pick up as Uber seeks to drive deeper into your life," *Financial Times,* November 3, 2016.

97 Fung, Esther, " Shopping Malls Are Tracking Your Every Move," *wsj.com,* March 14, 2017, https://wsj.com/articles/shopping-malls-are-tracking-uour-every-move-1489483800.

98 Manjoo, Farhad, "Maintaining Privacy in an Always-Watching Future," *The New York Times,* February 25, 2017.

99 Gapper, John, "Robots invest money better than people," *Financial Times,* March 17, 2016.

100 Hull, Dana and Hymowitz, Carol, "Will Seniors Be Robot Cars' Early Adopters?" *Bloomberg Businessweek,* March 7-13, 2016.

101 Corder, Charles, "Ready to give up the wheel?" *The Greenwood Commonwealth* (Mississippi), January 13, 2017.

102 Cookson, Clive, "Robot outperforms leading surgeons during US research," *Financial Times,* May 5, 2016. And, *The Economist,* "Who wields the knife? A machine carries out an operation almost unaided," May 7, 2016.

103 Rockoff, Jonathan D., "J&J Drops Its Sedasys Sedation Machine," *The Wall Street Journal,* March 15, 2016.

104 Akst, Daniel, "Algorithm Turns Cancer Sleuth," *The Wall Street Journal,* February 11-12, 2017.

105 Shekhtman, Lonnie, "Why do people blindly trust robot rescuers even when they're wrong?" *The Christian Science Monitor,* March 1, 2016.

106. Lloyd, Graham, Future Shocks, *The Australian*, January 28, 2017.
107. McGee, Patrick, "Cash-machine maker dispenses with pessimism. Diebold is so confident about the future that it is buying a German rival for $1.8 bn." *Financial Times*, April 7, 2016.
108. Hollinger, Peggy, "Meet the 'cobots': humans and robots learn how to work together on the factory floor. Collaborative machines are lighter, more flexible, easier to program and heading to a plant near you," *Financial Times, FT Special Series, Robots: Friend or Foe?* May 5, 2016.
109. *The 2017 IHG Trends Report*, IHG PLC, London, UK, January 2017.
110. Black, Jane, "Click Here for Healthy Meals. Eating your vegetables is getting easier all the time, thanks to new apps, delivery service and meal planners. We found these three especially tasty," *The Wall Street Journal*, April 3-0-May 1, 2016.
111. *Business Wire*, "Accenture Technology Vision 2017 Forecasts a Future of Technology for People, by People; Rapid acceleration of human-centric technology in AI, digital ecosystems and marketplaces will empower people, drive transformation of business and society," January 26, 2017.
112. *Dairy Foods*, "Balancing health and indulgence in frozen desserts," December 6, 2016
113. Ibid., December 6, 2016.
114. www.panerabread.com.
115. Light, Larry, and Kiddon, Joan, *Six Rules of Brand Revitalization: Learn the Most Common Mistakes and How to Avoid Them, Second Edition*, Pearson Education, Inc., Old Tappan, NJ, 2016, p. 59. See also, Whipp, Lindsay, "Nestlé Seeks to Defrost Growth from Frozen Foods: Group Bets on Shedding the Segment's 'Processed' Image with $50m Research Centre," *Financial Times*, July 22, 2015; and, Gretler, Corinne and Craig Giammona, "Nestlé Tries A Different Recipe for Lean Cuisine: It's Ditching the Frozen Food Brand's Focus on Calorie Counts: 'This is Not Going to Happen Overnight,'" *Bloomberg BusinessWeek*, June 29-July 5, 2015.
116. www.leancuisine.com.
117. www.purina.com.
118. *Global Wellness Institute*, http://www.globalwellnessinstitue.org/press-room/statistics-and-facts/
119. Canyon Ranch advertisement, *Travel & Leisure*, February 2017, 11.
120. Dougherty, Margot, "Om, the Places You'll Go!" *The Wall Street Journal*, December 31, 2016-January 1, 2017.
121. Baird, Kathleen, "Beauty gets the Uber treatment," *Financial Times*, February 11-12, 2017.

122 Lee, Jenny, "Scent by post: Florists who offer online subscription services cater for those who want flowers delivered all year round, not just Valentine's Day – and business is blooming," *Financial Times*, February 11-12, 2017.
123 PR Newswire, "Emerging Consciousness Economy™ Set to Make Purpose, Profit and Doing Good a Mainstream Brand Reality; JLJ Marketing publishes groundbreaking white paper on the rise of a self-awareness driven economy that's changing purchase decisions," September 27, 2016.
124 Op.cit., IHG, January 2017.
125 Johnson, Kate, "Gen Z Wants to Change the World," *Stylus*, December 7, 2015.
126 *Targeted News Service*, "Sabre identifies Asia Pacific Consumer Behaviours Driving Opportunities for Hotels in 2017," January 12, 2017.
127 Daniel, Diane, "In Transit: Q&A - Jared Steinberg uses tours to save people and places," *The New York Times*, December 18, 2016.
128 See The Futures Company, *Global Monitor 2013*.
129 Joseph, Marc, "The Blog: Do We Really Need to Volunteer," *Huffington Post*, February 2, 2017, http://www.huffingtonpost.com/marc-joseph/
130 *China Daily - US Edition*, "Learning by helping," January 25, 2017
131 Holland, Gwyneth, "Doing Good," *Stylus*, January 4, 2016.
132 Chen, Zengxiang, and Huang, Yunhui, "Cause-related marketing is not always less favorable than corporate philanthropy: The moderating role of self-construal," *International Journal of Research in Marketing*, Vol. 33, 2016, pp. 868-880.
133 *The Economist 1843*, April-May 2017, p. 62.
134 Bahl, Sahlini; Milne, George R.; Ross, Spencer M.; Mick, David Glen; Grier, Sonya A.; Chugani, Sunaina K.; Chan, Steven S.; Gould, Stephen; Cho, Yoon-Na; Dorsey, Joshua D.; Schindler, Robert M.; Murdock, Mitchel R.; and Boesen-Mariani, Sabine, "Mindfulness: Its Transformative Potential for Consumer, Societal, and Environmental Well-Being," *Journal of Public Policy and Marketing*, Fall 2016.
135 Raz, Nicole, "Local Companies Stepping Up Philanthropic Giving," *Las Vegas Review-Journal*, February 11, 2017; and also see, *Foreign Direct Investment*, Cover Story: The Millennial Effect, *Financial Times Ltd*, December 1, 2015. Also, DeViincenzo, Marie Hafey and Scammon, Debra, "Principle-Based Consumption Communities: Exploring the Meanings from Socially Conscious Consumption Practices, *Journal of Public Policy & Marketing,* Fall 2015.
136 Walt, Vivian, "Selling Soap and Saving the World," *Forbes*, March 1, 2017, pp. 122-130.

137 Jennings, Lisa, "Kimbal Musk's Next Door Concept Builds Local Supply" 'Real food' restaurant plans 50 new units across America's heartland," *Restaurant- Hospitality*, March 2017, pp. 18-19.

138 All advertisements appear in *The New York Times Style Review*, February 19, 2017; Chantecaille, p. 137; emeco.net, p. 149; Gemfields, p. 167; www.gudrunsjoden.com, p. 179.

139 Dadderio, Luciana, "The project management paradox: dependable innovation," *University of Strathclyde Business School website* http://www.engage-sbs.co/project-management-paradox/, April 9, 2015.

140 *Business Monitor Online*, "CES Announcements Highlight Connected Car Trends," January 9, 2017.

141 *Business Wire*, "Ford, Samsung Integrate SYNC with Samsung Gear S2 and S3 to Help Drivers Mark and Find Parking Spots, Stay Alert," January 4, 2017.

142 *Marketing News Publishing*, "Panasonic Countertop Induction Oven Selected as CES 2017 Innovation Award Honoree," January4, 2017.

143 *ICT Monitor Worldwide*, "World's First Automatic Grill-Cleaning Robot to Debut new Bluetooth-enabled Grillbot Pro at CES," January 6, 2017.

144 *Euromonitor International*, 2014 Report. Also see, www.euromonitor.com.

145 *PR Newswire Asia*, "Volvo Cars' Concierge Service Will Make Your Life Easier," November 17, 2016.

146 *Business Wire*, "TomTom Press Statement," December 2, 2016.

147 Murphy, Kate, "Why Help on Tech is Unbearable," *The New York Times*, July 4, 2016.

148 Kaneman, D., and Tversky, A., "Prospect Theory: An analysis of decision under risk," *Econometrics*, 1979, Vol. 47, pp. 263-291. And also, Zeni, Thomas A.; Buckley, M. Ronald; Mumford, Michael D., and Griffith, Jennifer A., "Making sense of ethical decision making," *The Leadership Quarterly*, 2016, Vol. 27, pp. 838-855.

149 Op. cit, *Global Monitor*, 2013.

150 http://www.endlessturns.com

151 http://www.devlopingworldconnections.com

152 Levere, Janet, "A Virtual Trip Before, or Instead of, Real Travel," *The New York Times*, February 13, 2017.

153 *Travel & Leisure Close-Up*, "The Arena Launches at Kalahari Resorts and Conventions," newsdesk@closeupmedia.com; http://www.KalahariResorts.com.

154 Mangione, Nick, "Adventure Time: Islands Reveals Where the Humans Went and It's Eerily Plausible," *Geek.com*, February 2, 2017.

155 *ENP Newswire*, "Venture into The Wild at ARTSCIENCE MUSEUM; A Collaboration with Google, Lenovo and WWF," February 9, 2017.
156 Jones, Sarah, "Jimmy Choo Engages in Risky Behavior to Launch Illicit," *Luxury Daily*, September 3, 2015, http://www.luxurydaily.com.
157 Iliff, Laurence, "Amid sales push, RAV4 goes in a more rugged direction," *Automotive News*, February 13, 2017.
158 https://mic.com/articles/2870/why-64-of-americans-have-never-left-the-u-s.
159 Snow, Blake, "Off the Grid: Why Americans Don't Travel Abroad," www.pastemagazine.com, April 14, 2016.

PART 3: PRINCIPLES FOR FINDING PARADOXES AND GENERATING PARADOX PROMISES

160 Nagl, John A., *Learning to Eat Soup with a Knife: Counterinsurgency Lessons from Malaya and Vietnam*, 2002.
161 Gardner, Howard, *Five Minds for the Future*, Harvard Business Press, 2007. Also see, https://howardgardner.com/five-minds-for-the-future/, and, *HRB IdeaCast* interview, Paul Michelman host, Steve Singer, interviewer and Howard Gardner, interviewee; April 5, 2007.
162 Gardner, Howard, "Five Minds for the Future," oral presentation at the Ecolint Meeting, Geneva, Switzerland, January 14, 2008.
163 Op.cit. Light and Kiddon, 2016, 109.
164 Op. cit., Gardner, 2008.
165 Hirshberg, Jerry, *The Creative Priority: Putting Innovation to Work in Your Business*, HarperCollins, 1998.
166 Levitt, Theodore, "Creativity is Not Enough," *Harvard Business Review*, August, 2002; also see http://www.azquotes.com/author/21653-Theodore_Levitt.
167 *Singapore Straits*, February 14, 2017.
168 Op. cit., Light and Kiddon, 2016, p. 191.
169 Beer, Michael, and Nohira, Nitin, "Cracking the Code of Change," *Harvard Business Review*, May-June 2000; and, *Harvard Business Review on Turnarounds*, Harvard Business School Press, 1997. Theory E focuses on maximizing shareholder value through top down leadership with plans, programs, structures and systems. Financial incentives motivate managers. Theory O focuses on developing enterprise proficiencies in a bottom-up approach with an emphasis on culture, behaviors, attitudes, and experiments. The idea is to make employees advocates for the organization rather than express acquiescence.

170. Vahlnea, Jan-Erik, and Jonssonb, Anna, "Ambidexterity as a dynamic capability in the globalization of the multinational business enterprise (MBE): Case studies of AB Volvo and IKEA," *International Business Review*, Vol. 26, 2017, 57-70.
171. The Supremes, "You Can't Hurry Love, *Motown Label*, Holland-Dozier-Holland, 1966.

PART 4: LESSONS FROM CREATING PARADOX PROMISES

172. *Dairy Foods*, "Balancing health and indulgence in frozen desserts," BNP Media, December 6, 2016.
173. See Dawn Dishwashing Liquid website, www.dawn-dish.com/en-us.
174. Pooler, Michael, "Hauling construction into the sharing economy," The Monday Interview, *Financial Times*, April 17, 2017.
175. Pine, B. Joseph II, and Gilmore, James H., "Welcome to the Experience Economy," *Harvard Business Review*, July-August, 1988.
176. Op. cit., Light and Kiddon, 2015.
177. Ibid., 194.
178. Ibid., 188.
179. See Doz, Yves, and Kosonen, Mikko, "The Dynamics of Strategic Agility: Nokia's Rollercoaster Experience," *California Management Review*, Vol. 50. No. 3, Spring 2008.
180. Op. cit., Light, and Kiddon, 2016.
181. Ibid., Light and Kiddon, 2016.
182. See discussion in Day, George and Fahey, Liam, "Valuing Market Strategies," *Marketing Science Institute*, 1988.
183. *Athleta Catalogue*, February 2017.
184. https://www.unilever.com/sustainable-living/
185. See de la Merced, Michael J., and Bray, Chad, "Kraft Heinz Withdraws Takeover Bid For Unilever," *The New York Times*, February 20, 2017.
186. http://www.wholefoodsmarket.com/mission-values/core-values
187. We have discussions about Internal Marketing in two of our (Light and Kiddon) previous books: *Six Rules for Brand Revitalization*, 2009, and in *Six Rules of Brand Revitalization: Second Edition*, 2016.
188. Op. cit., Light and Kiddon, 2015, 76.
189. www.ihgplc.com, and, op. cit., Light and Kiddon, 2016.
190. Op. cit., Light and Kiddon, 2016, 170.
191. Levitt, Theodore, "Marketing Myopia," *Harvard Business Review*, July-August 1960.

INDEX

A

AB InBev, 53
"abundant rarity," 34
Accenture report, 50–51
accountability
    avoidance of, 14, 117
    lack of, 118
    as sacrificed on altar of measurement, 100
    shift in, 50
Adventure Time (TV series), 74
aesthetician treatments, 54
Age of Anger: A History of The Present (Mishra), xiii
The Age of I (2017), xiii, xv, 5–12, 15, 16, 24, 56, 59, 111, 120, 122, 131
Age of Me (1960s and 1970s), xiii, 8, 9, 17
Age of We (1950s), xiii
Airbnb, 23, 27
Airbus airplanes, 49
Alessi, 37
Alexa personal assistant, 40
algorithms, 26, 38, 39, 41, 45, 46, 47, 49, 100
alienation
    social media as generating feeling of, xiii
    as uniting people into powerful political force, 1
alone and together paradox, 24–27
"alone together" paradox, 6
Altamont, 8
Amazon, 38, 40, 66, 67–68, 107
American Express, 35
American grocery stores, ease of choice in, 66
American presidential election (2016), 1, 8
Amish, 10
anesthesiologists, 47
anger
    causes of, 3
    countries on trajectory of, xiii
Anna (Duchess of Bedford), 32
Apple, xii, 30, 40, 67, 111
apple candy example, 96
apps
    Houseparty, 6
    for ordering on-demand spa, hair salon, nail salon services, etc., 55
    for parking spaces, 64

Sweetgreen, 50
    use of to avoid "sinking feeling," 32
The Arena, 74
Armani Jeans, 36
Armani Junior, 36
Arnold, Chris, 124
arrogance of success, 119–120
artificial intelligence, 40, 41, 44, 47, 48, 49
"artisanal globalisation," 12
ArtScience Museum (Singapore), 74–75
ASDA, 97
Ashtead, 113
ask "Is this actionable?" as principle for finding paradoxes, 94–96
Athleta, 122
"ATM experience," 49
automation, 39, 40, 41, 46
automotive brands, 36, 41
Automotive News, 76
autonomous vehicles, 46–47
avoidance mechanism, 4
A/X brand, 36

B

Baby Boomers, 41, 46
balance, defined, xvi, 17
be a runway not a control tower, as principle for finding paradoxes, 96–99
Beachbody, 23
Beale, Howard (character in *Network*), xi, xiii, xvi, 3
Bell, Charlie, 97
belonging
    as clickable not touchable, 10
    craving for shared belonging, 7
    as everything, post-World War II, 8
    as having benefits, 11
    importance of, 5
    as innate human desire, 9
    personal status and, 35
    searching for, 26
    wanting both distinctiveness and, 9, 15
Bernstein, Jacob, 6, 9
BlaBlaCar, 112
Black Opium fragrance, 75
Bloomberg BusinessWeek, 46
Bloomberg TV, 122
Blue Apron, 50
Bluetooth, 65
Botox®, 54
BP, 71
brand academy example, 98
brand experience
    building exclusivity into, 37
    consumers as assessing brand's worth based on, 128
    defined, 113
    importance of being clear, understandable, and valuable, 37
    importance of being relevant, differentiating, trustworthy, 79
    importance of creating extraordinary trustworthy, valued, 17, 113
    individualizing, 6
    Paradox Promise as creating, 127
    as tied up with customer's perception of brand's

trustworthy brand value, 127
Brand Journalism, 114
brand-business social responsibility, 122
Brexit vote, 1, 8
Bring on The Beer, 36
British Airways, example of global-central approach, 13
Brookings Institution, 42
Brooks, David, xiv, 3

C

cable and mobile service companies, behavior and attitudes at, 69
Cadillac, 30
Camel cigarettes, 81, 82
Camp Grounded, 22
Cantalupo, Jim, 97
Canyon Ranch®, 54–55
Carnegie Hall, 32
Carney, Mark, 11
Carnival Cruise Line's, Fathom™ brand, 57
cars
    automotive brands, 36, 41
    autonomous vehicles, 46–47
Cartoon Network, 74
cause-related marketing, 59
Cayla (Internet-enabled doll), 43
CES (Consumer Electronic Show), 40, 64
Chanel, 34, 36
Chantecaille, 61, 75
chatbot, 23
Chayefsky, Paddy, xi–xii, 16
Chief Marketing Officer (CMO), 120–121

China, "voluntourism" (volunteer tourism), 57–58
Chipotle, 52, 53, 71, 124
chocolate fill bar example, 83–84
ClassPass, 23
"clean" foods, 52, 53
Clinique, 16
CloudPets™, 43
Club Med, 22
Coach, 34–35
coffee, as drink of choice for younger generations, 32
Cohen, Roger, 24
collaboration
    importance of, 116–118
    origin of word, 116
    welcoming of, 68
The Collaborative Three-Box Model, 13, 116, 117
Collins, James C., 3
collision of globalizing, localizing, and personalizing forces, xv, 5, 12–16, 111, 131–132
Colvin, Geoff, 39–40
communal working spaces, 23
communes (1960s), 10
communications
    between humans and machines, 26
    between machines, 26
community
    belonging to, 15
    Club Med as social community, 22
    elderly faring better in, 58
    "virtual" community, 23
concert events, nostalgia affecting, 32

conference calling, 21
conflicting needs, xiv, xv, 3, 18, 32
conformity, era of (1950s), 7–8
"connected aloneness," 25
connection and disconnection
    paradox, 21–24
connection-disconnection-
    reconnection, 23
Consciousness Economy, 56, 60
constant sum contests, xvi, 17
Consumer Electronic Show (CES),
    40, 64
Consumption with a Conscience, 60
"contact," being a, 23
continuous positive
    reinforcement, 26
contradictions
    living in world of, xiv, 1
    "managing the
        contradictions," 97
contradictory needs, xiv, 3, 10, 17,
    21, 30, 79, 111
conversation, replacements for, 26
corporate philanthropy, 59
corporate social responsibility (CSR),
    58, 59, 122, 123
Cortana personal assistant, 40, 42
craft beer, 36–37, 53
Creating Mind, 83
creative abrasion, 90
creative tensions, as strategic
    drivers, 3
creativity, 48, 79, 85, 90–92, 93,
    100, 113–114, 115, 116
The Crisis of the Middle Class, 2
Crowne Plaza WorkLife Room
    example, 87–88
CSR (corporate social responsibility),
    58, 59, 122, 123

Cullen, Bill, 127
culture, as winner over strategy, 107
customer perceived value, 127, 128

D

Da Vinci, Leonardo, 80
Dadderio, Luciana, 62–63
The Daily Telegraph, 31
Dairy Foods magazine, 52
Daniel, Diane, 57
The Dartmouth, 25
Darwin, Charles, 83
Dauke, David, 96
Dawn dishwashing liquid, 112
de Clapiers, Luc, 82
death, online conservations after, 23
decision-making
    as done by people not
        processes, 101
    "gains" rather than "losses,"
        70–71
    as more difficult than ever, 65
    overload, 65
    satisficing as strategy for, 71–72
delay and desire paradox, 27–30
demographics, 1, 85
dependability, defined, 63
dependable innovation, 62
DePillis, Lydia, 34
Developing World Connections, 73
devices, obsession with, 24
Diebold, 49
Diet and Delight paradox, 52, 54
Diet Coke, 111
differentiate information from trends
    from insights, as principle for
    finding paradoxes, 85–89
"digital depression," 25
Digital Detox, 22

digitization, xiii, 15, 39
Dior, 75
Disciplinary Mind, 82–83
discipline
    and freedom, 90–91
    importance of, 118–119
Discover Card, 39
dishwashing liquid paradox, 112
Disney, 73
diversity, benefits of, xvi
Do It for Me in My Way and Do It for Myself, 50
do not fall for the killer question, as principle for finding paradoxes, 103–106
"doing good for me" and "doing good for the planet" paradox, 59
domestic travel, preference for, 76
Doz, Yves, 119
Drabble, Geoff, 113
Dunlop, Al ("Chainsaw"), 97
Dylan, Bob, 84
Dyson, 88–89
Dyson, James, 116
Dysport®, 54

E

ease of choice, as one of Three Dimensions of Ease, 65–67
ease of mind, as one of Three Dimensions of Ease, 70–71
ease of use, as one of Three Dimensions of Ease, 67–70
Easterbrook, Gregg, xii–xiii
"easy-to-use," 64
Echo, 42
eco-consciousness, 58
The Economist 1843, 59
The Economist, 14, 37, 38

Edelman, 126
education, organizational, 98
eHarmony, 49
eight Ps, 119
1980s, 127–128
85% rule example, 101–102
elitism, 2
Ells, Steve, 124
emeco.net, 61
emotional decisions, handling of, 39
Employee Stock Ownership Plan (ESOP) program, 13
Endless Turns, 72–73
Erewhon Natural Food stores, 51
Erhard, Werner, 8
est (Erhard Seminars Training), 8
Eternime, 23
ethical dilemmas/issues, 49, 51, 57, 70
Ethical Mind, 83
Etsy, 30
Euromonitor International, 65
European appliance company example, 88–89
European Union (EU), 11
exclusive and affordable paradox, 36–38
Exxon, 71
E-ZPass®, 41

F

Face Time, 21
Facebook, 43, 45, 49
families
    kin families, 10
    kindred families, 10
fandom, 25
fashion and art nostalgia, 32
fashion industry

affording chance to feel adventurous, 75
creating different lines to protect ultimate luxury offering, 36
example of planet-loving behaviors in, 59
and pollution, 59
feel good by doing good, 61–62
Ferdman, Roberto, 31
fifties (1950s), 8, 37
fight the hypnosis of the measurement mystique, as principle for finding paradoxes, 99–103
fillers, 54
financial capital, 126
financial investment, 45
Financial Times, 33, 41, 44, 45, 55, 113
"fintech" companies, 39
five action Ps, 124
Five Minds for the Future (Gardner), 82
flower arrangements, 55
food awakening, 33
food industry, 33, 51–54, 66
Forbes, 22
Ford/Ford Motor Company, 36, 46, 62, 64, 107
formulated creativity, 92
Fortune, 39
fragrance industry, 75
France, "right to disconnect" law, 22
Franklin, Benjamin, 31
The Franklin Mint, 111
freedom, discipline and, 90–91
Freedom within a Framework, 91, 113–114
Fresh Direct, 50
friendship, virtual approach to, 23
frozen dairy desserts category, 52, 112
frustration
 as breeding anger, xiv
 current state of, xiii
The Futures Company, 2, 71

G

Gap Inc., 122
Garbo, Greta, 44
Gardner, Howard, 82–83, 90
Garfield, Simon, 31
Gathered Table, 50
GE, 98, 107
Gemalto, 43
Gemfields, 61
General Electric, 88
Generation X, 39
Generzation Z, xiv, 6, 56
"Genius of the AND," 4
Gernert, Greg, 26–27
"gig" economy, 23
Gilmore, James H., 113
Giorgio Armani, 36
Giorgio Armani Privé, 36
Givenchy, 28
global brands
 contending with three-way tug of war, 13, 15–16
 "enraged" people not buying products and services from, 2
 management of, 116
Global Entry, 62, 63
Global Monitor, 2–3, 71
global segmentation study, 92
The Global Wellness Institute, 54

global-central approach, 13
globalization
    "artisanal globalisation," 12
    global economy, 11
Google, 40, 107
Google Now personal assistant, 40
Gore-Tex, 111
GPS system, 48
GQ magazine, 31
The Great Funk (Hine), 8
green-speak (green-washing), 58
The Greenwood Commonwealth, 46
Grillbot Pro, 65
"guest journeys," 50
Gundrun Sjödén, 61–62
Gyllenhammar, Pehr, 103–104

H

Hanson, Tim, 35
Harvard Business Review, 97
Hasbro, 49
headphones, obsession with, 24
Hello Barbie products, 43
Henry (High Earner Not Rich Yet), 39
heritage credibility, 33
Hermes, 34
Hine, Thomas, 8
Hirschberg, Jerry, 90
home purchase, Millennials as shunning, 67
hospitality industry
    "betterment," 56
    maximizing Do It for Me in My Way and Do It for Myself, 50
    satisfying need to connect and need to be disconnected, 27

hotels, 41, 58
Houseparty (app), 6
how to smile example, 102
Howard Johnson's (HoJo's), 37–38
Huffington Post, 57
human capital, 126
human voice, replacements for, 26
"human-centered technology," 51
Hygge, 31
hyper-connected, 21

I

"I Used To Be Human" (Sullivan), 23
IBM, 107, 115
identity
    multiple identities, 6
    self-identity, 6
    sense of, 15
identity politics, 1
IHG, 87
IHG 2015 Trends Report, 126
IHG Report, 50
Illicit fragrance, 75
impact travel, 57
importance of collaboration, as lesson from creating Paradox Promises, 116–118
importance of discipline, as lesson from creating Paradox Promises, 118–119
importance of freedom within a framework, as lesson from creating Paradox Promises, 113–114
importance of internal marketing, as lesson from creating Paradox Promises, 124–125

importance of marketing, as lesson from creating Paradox Promises, 120–121
importance of organizational diversity of thinking, as lesson from creating Paradox Promises, 115–116
importance of standing up for what you stand for, as lesson from creating Paradox Promises, 122–124
importance of strategic dexterity, as lesson from creating Paradox Promises, 119–120
importance of the paradox promise, as lesson from creating Paradox Promises, 111–113
importance of trust, as lesson from creating Paradox Promises, 126–127
importance of trustworthy brand value, as lesson from creating Paradox Promises, 127–128
improved me and improved we paradox, 56–62, 122
inclusivity, need for, 5, 17
individual and interdependent paradox, 59
individualism
    need for, 5
    networked individualism, 9
individuality, need for, 17
indulgence, origin of word, 55
indulgence and wellness paradox, 51–56
industrial problem detection example, 104–105
information, relationship with trends, 85
information overload, 65
innovation, dependable, 62
innovative and dependable paradox, 62–65, 70
insights
    criteria of, 87
    defined, 86
    as marketing cliché, 86
    relationship with trends, 85
    templates for, 92–93
instant gratification, xiv
institutional trust, status of, 2
Intel, 46
intellectual capital, 126
"intentional" communities, 10
internal marketing
    importance of, 124–125
    parts of, 125
    rules of, 125
Internet
    allowing maximization of desire and delay, 29
    creating society of "connected aloneness" and "digital depression," 25
intimate isolation, 25
Into the Wild exhibit, 75
invisible technologies, 50
isolation, domestic needs, 11

J

Jack Daniels, 33
Jaguar, 62
Japanese luxury vehicle example, 105–106
Jim Beam, 33
Jimmy Choo, 75
Johnnie Walker Scotch, 35
Johnson, Howard, 38

Johnson & Johnson, 47
journalism, described, 114
"Joy for All" kitty cat (Hasbro), 49
Junior Mermaid Camp, 73

K

Kalahari Resorts and
    Conventions, 74
Kapferer, Jean-Noël, 34
Katharine Hammett, 59
Kellogg, 119–120
Kent State killings, 8
Kering, 59
KFC, 14, 33
Kik, 21
Kirk, Captain (character on *Star Trek*), 48
Kosonen, Mikko, 119
Kraft Heinz, 123
Kroc, Ray, 107, 116

L

LA fitness scene, 23
Lagerfeld, Karl, 28
language, importance of, 85
Lava Sauce (Taco Bell), 36
Le Pavillion restaurant, 38
Le Wild fragrance, 75
Lean Cuisine, 53–54
lessons from creating Paradox
    Promises, 111–129
Levere, Janet, 73
Levi's, 30–31
Levitt, Theodore, 13, 14, 94, 127
Lexus, 36
Like button, 25
limited time options (LTOs), 36
LinkedIn, 45
"living in the web," 23
loneliness, of Americans, 25
look for ideas outside of your
    standard social media circles,
    favorite periodicals, e-zines,
    information sites and journals,
    as principle for finding
    paradoxes, 82–85
look for the little things, as principle
    for finding paradoxes, 80–82
Louis Vuitton, 34
loyalty clubs, 38
LTOs (limited time options), 36
luxury
    "democratization" of, 35
    new concept of, 34
    traditional concept of, 34
luxury couture industry, 27–28, 30
LVMH, 59
Lyft, 112

M

"managing the contradictions," 97
marketing
    cause-related marketing, 59
    importance of, 120–121
    internal marketing, 124–125
    as more customized,
        individualized, and
        personalized, 15
    one theme marketing, 14
marketing discipline, 101
Marlboro cigarettes, 81–82
Marriott, 23
massages, 54
match.com, 49
*Material Girls, Mystical World: The
    Now Age Guide to a High Vibe
    Life* (Warrington), 33

McDonald's, 14, 36, 84, 95, 97, 102, 106–107, 114, 116
McRib, 36
measurement, role of, 99–100
medicine, "non-human-in-charge," 47
Mercury, 36
metrics, use of, 100–101
"microholidays," 23
Microsoft, 40, 62
Millennials, xiv, 6, 33, 39, 41, 61, 67, 86
Miller, Richard, 9
Miller Beer, 81
Miller Lite, 53, 111
Mims, Christopher, 6
mindfulness, 59–60
mindless consumption, 59–60
Mishra, Pankaj, xiii
Missoni, 37
Mobley, Esther, 37
monastic-type, faith-based communities, as recent trend in US, 10
Monterey Pop music festival, 32
Moravec, Hans, 50
Motley Fool, 35
Motorola, 98
Muhlke, Christine, 33
multiple "accessible selves," 6
multiple identities, 6
Murphy, Kate, 69
Musk, Kimbal, 61

N

Nagl, John, 80
nationalism, 11
nativism, 11
Nestlé, 53–54
Network (film), xi, 16
networked individualism, 9
networked narcissism, 9
New Brand Leadership (Light and Kiddon), 9, 13, 116
"The New Classic Cars, Are Younger than You Think," 31
new product development process, 91
New York (magazine), 25
The New York Times Book Review, 31
New York Times Style Review, 61
The New York Times, xiv–xv, 6, 22, 33, 37, 38, 42, 57, 69
newspaper example, 80–81
Next Door restaurant concept, 61
Nike, 28
1950s, 8, 37
1970s, 16, 75, 81, 84, 88
1976, events of, xii
1960s, 10, 38, 75, 127
1990s, 51, 63
Nissan Xterra, 75
Nixon, Richard, 8
"non-human-in-charge," 47
non-linear thinking, 82–83
NordicTrack x 22i Incline Trainer, 23
nostalgia
    affecting concert events, 32
    fashion and art nostalgia, 32
    origin of word, 32

O

old is new, 33
On the Origin of the Species (Darwin), 83
one million dollars a customer example, 102–103
online communities, impact of, 5

online grocery shopping, 29–30
online relationships, impermanence of, 26
organizational diversity of thinking, importance of, 115–116
organizational education, 98
organizations, expected to be "good-doers," 58
OTAs, 50

P

PACE program, 122
Pally, Marcia, 9
Panasonic, 64
Panera Bread, 52–53
Paradox Promises, xv, xvi, 12, 17, 18, 41, 47, 79, 96, 100, 111, 121, 125, 132
paradoxes
    alone and together, 24–27
    connection and disconnection, 21–24
    delay and desire, 27–30
    diet and delight, 52, 54
    dishwashing liquid, 112
    "doing good for me" and "doing good for the planet," 59
    exclusive and affordable, 36–38
    importance of understanding, 3
    improved me and improved we, 56–62, 122
    independent/connected force of The Age of I, 10
    individual and interdependent paradox, 59
    indulgence and wellness, 51–56
    innovative and dependable, 62–65, 70
    living in world of, xiv
    of McDonald's brand, 84–85
    as multi-dimensional, 21
    as outcome of uncertainty, 131
    "paradox of the headphone experience," 9
    within paradoxes, 21
    personalization (automated) and personal (human), 38–41
    preserving anonymity and wanting to be known, 41
    principles for finding and generating Paradox Promises, 79–108
    privacy and personalization, 41–45
    relief and unease, 104
    safe and adventure, 72–76
    simplicity and complexity, 104
    technological control and human control, 45–51
    technology and comfort, 63, 70
    timeliness and timelessness, 30–36
parallel societies, 1
passports, percent of Americans having, 76
Patagonia®, 59
PearsonLloyd, 88
Peleton, 23
People
    as one of eight Ps, 119
    as one of five action Ps, 124
People's Park in Berkeley, 8
Perfect (film), 23
Performance as one of eight Ps, 119
personal assistants, 40
personal information, giving away of, 41–44
"personal" messages, 38–39

personalization (automated) and personal (human) paradox, 38–41
"personalization engine," 40
personalized experiences, 16
personalizing, force of, 15
Philip Morris, 81
Pierre Cardin, 35
Piggly Wiggly, 52
Pinault, François-Henri, 28
Pine, B. Joseph, II, 113
Place
    as one of eight Ps, 119
    as one of five action Ps, 124
Plan to Win, 118–119, 120
plastic surgery, 54
Plated, 50
polarization
    as affecting business and brands, 2
    global malaise of, xiii
    as grasping institutions and beliefs, 1
Pollman, Paul, 61
populism, 1, 2, 3
Porras, Jerry I., 3
"positioning," as outdated, 18
posture-challenged people, 24
preserving anonymity and wanting to be known paradox, 41
Price
    as one of eight Ps, 119
    as one of five action Ps, 124
The Price is Right (TV show), 127
Principle-Based or Purposeful Consumption, 60–61
principles for finding paradoxes, 79–108
privacy

conundrum of, 42
erosion of, 41
privacy and personalization paradox, 41–45
The Privacy Paradox, 42
Products
    as one of eight Ps, 119
    as one of five action Ps, 124
Prokopec, Sonja, 35
Promise, as one of eight Ps, 119
Promotion
    as one of eight Ps, 119
    as one of five action Ps, 124
Prospect Theory, 70–71
Publix Supermarket, 13
Purina, 54
Purple Carrot, 50
Purpose, as one of eight Ps, 119

R

Rachman, Gideon, 2
Reagan, Ronald, 9
real time, xiv, 21, 27, 31, 74
recession (2008), effects of, 1
relief and unease paradox, 104
Rent-the-Runway, 112
"re-orgs," 98
restaurant industry, 33, 51
"retro" move, in financial services, 46
Return on Global Learning (ROGL), 117
"right to disconnect" law, 22
robotics, 26, 39, 41, 45, 46, 47, 48, 49, 50, 51, 65
role of culture example, 107–108

S

Sabre Corporation, 56

"safe adventure travel," 72–73
safe and adventure paradox, 72–76
Salvador, Freda, 28–29
Samsung, 62, 64
San Francisco Chronicle, 37
"satisficing," 71
Sauvage fragrance, 75
Scott Paper, 97
SeaWorld, 73
Sedasys sedation machine, 47
segregated online communities, 26
self-identity, 6
selfie-celeb connected culture, 9
selfies, 25
self-regulation, 60
self-satisfaction and selflessness paradox, 56
"separability and situatedness," 9
separateness, 11
seventies (1970s), 16, 75, 81, 84, 88
The Shamu Experience, 73
sharing economy, 67, 87, 112
silos, cautions with, 118
Simon, Herbert, 71
simplicity and complexity paradox, 104
Singapore, ArtScience Museum, 74–75
"sinking feeling," 32
Sirens of the Deep Mermaid Camp, 73
Siri personal assistant, 40
Six Rules of Brand Revitalization, Second Edition (Light and Kiddon), 96, 119
sixties (1960s), 10, 38, 75, 127
Skapinker, Michael, 2
"skunk works," 115
Skype, 21

smart home, 63–64, 95–96
smartphones, 22, 44, 62, 66
social animals, people as, 7
social media
    avenues for disconnected connections, 23
    as giving people very loud voice, 57
    impact of culture of, xiii
social responsibility, 122. *See also* corporate social responsibility (CSR)
Socially Conscious Consumption, 60
SoFi, 39
solidarity, 11
spa treatments, 54
Spock, Dr. (character on *Star Trek*), 48
standardized, centralized, one theme marketing, 14
standing up for what you stand for, importance of, 122–124
Star Trek (TV series), 48
Starbucks, 6
start-up companies, development focus in, 4
Stein, Sadie, 32
Steinberg, Jared, 56–57
Stella McCartney, 59
strategic dexterity, importance of, 119–120
Sullivan, Andrew, 23
The Summer of Love, 32, 127
SunPass, 41
surgical robots, 47
SUVs, 75
Sweetgreen (app), 50
SwimTrek ®, 55
swiping, 25, 49

Sx Rules of Brand Revitalization, Second Edition (Light and Kiddon), 53
SXSW Festival (2017), 7
synthesis
    defined, 86
    requirements for, 106
Synthesizing Mind, 83

T

Taco Bell, 36
Takata, 71
Target, 37
Tata, 62
tax preparation services, 68–69
teatime concept, demise of, 31–32
techdirt, 43
"tech-laden" toys, 43
technological control and human control paradox, 45–51
technology and comfort paradox, 63, 70
"Technology for People" report, 51
tension
    between belonging to something bigger and independence, 11
    creative tensions as strategic drives, 3
    creativity as involving, 90
    generated by zero-sum situations, xiii
    between immediacy and waiting, 27
    as leading to original thinking, 114
    marketing as inherently having, 121
    between need to belong and need to have unique identity, 5, 131
    privacy-personalization tension, 45
    between real selves and digital selves, real families and digital families, 10
    between regions and center, 15, 117
    of ubiquity and exclusivity, 35
Terms of Endearment (film), 25
Tesla, 29, 46, 62
testing, role of, 101
Theory E schema of change, 97
Theory O schema of change, 97
there is no formula for creative thinking, as principle for finding paradoxes, 90–93
Think Global. Act Local. (TGAL), 14–15
ThinkPad group (IBM), 115
This Is Us (TV show), 25
Thornhill, John, 41
Three Dimensions of Ease, 65–72
3M, 91
time, as precious resource, 31
timeliness and timelessness paradox, 30–36
Tinder, 49
Tisci, Riccardo, 28
TomTom, 69
too much change example, 98–99
toy company example, 91–93
Toyota, 36
Toyota RAV4, 75–76
trade-off approach, 3
trade-off decisions, 4, 12, 39, 48
trade-off solutions, 4

trade-offs, 4, 40, 131
transponder toll payment systems, 41–42
Travel and Leisure magazine, 54
trends
    defined, 85–86
    relationship with information and insights, 85
trust
    as affecting loyalty, 126
    importance of, 126–127
    role of in maximization of personalization and privacy, 42
    role of in optimizing paradox promises, 47–48
Trust Barometer, 126
trust capital, 126–127
trustworthy brand value, importance of, 127–128
Trustworthy Brand Value™ equation, 128
Turner, Fred, 116
TV watching, as interactive, connective, streaming, 22–23
The 2017 IHG Trends Report, 50
The 2016 Edelman Trust Barometer, 2
Tylman-Mikiewicz, Anders, 68
"Tyranny of the OR," 3

U

Uber, 23, 44, 46, 55
ubiquitous technology, impact of, 5
unbalance, current state of, xiii
"the Un-Googleables, the online elusive ones," 42
Unilever, 123
United Airlines, 71
United Nations, resolutions, 11

United States Customs and Border Patrol, 63
United States Postal Service, 40
"urban casual" environment, 61
USAA, 39

V

vacationing, volunteering while, 57, 73
Vietnam War, 8
virtual (VR) reality, 73–74
"virtual" community, 23
virtual reality gaming and experience business, 73
virtual worlds, 25
Vivienne Westwood, 59
Vizio TV, 42
Volkswagen, 72
Voltaire, xiii
volunteering, while vacationing, 57, 73
"voluntourism" (volunteer tourism), 57–58
Volvo, 68
Vtech, 43

W

The Wall Street Journal, 43, 47, 55
Wal-Mart, 52
Warrington, Ruby, 33
washingtonpost.com, 34
Weeki Wachee Springs State Park (Florida), 73
WEF Davos, 2, 49
"Welcome to the Experience Economy" (Pine and Gilmore), 113
wellness industry, 54–56
Westin, 23

WeWork, 7, 23
Whole Foods Market®, 51–52, 123–124
Wild Attitude fragrance, 75
Wildfitness® Boot Camp, 55
wine industry, 37
Wolf, Martin, 2
"workout" culture (1980s), 23
Wyndham Hotels, 38

Y

yoga vacations, 55
you can't hurry love, as principle for finding paradoxes, 106–108
Yves Saint Laurent, 75

Z

Zenbanx, 39
zero-sum situations, xiii, xiv, 11, 12

www.ingramcontent.com/pod-product-compliance
Lightning Source LLC
Chambersburg PA
CBHW032014170526
45157CB00002B/695